Contents

ArcGIS® 9

What is ArcGIS® 9.1?

GIS concepts and requirements

> **"GIS is evolving from a database approach to a knowledge approach."**
>
> *ESRI President Jack Dangermond*

Knowledge is shared through many abstract forms. Attempts to articulate and explain human experience and understanding use these abstractions—summaries of a larger body of knowledge. Abstractions, such as text, hieroglyphics, language, mathematics and statistics, music and art, drawings, images, and maps, are used to record and communicate experiences, culture, and history from generation to generation.

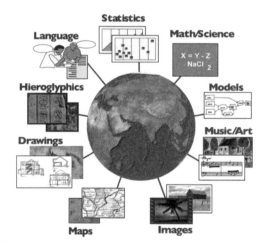

Many abstractions are used to communicate the understanding of the earth and its systems. Geography provides a universal framework for abstraction and communication of "place.".

Digital computing allows the capture and sharing of knowledge across networks such as the Internet. Simultaneously, geographic information system (GIS) technology is evolving and provides better methods to understand, represent, manage, and communicate the many aspects of the earth as a system.

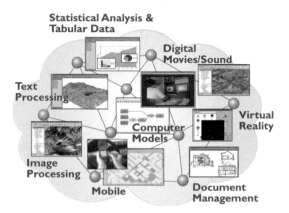

Digital technology is increasingly used to capture, share, and store knowledge.

Geography has traditionally provided an important framework and language for organizing and communicating key concepts about the world.

FIVE ELEMENTS OF GEOGRAPHIC KNOWLEDGE

GIS provides a comparatively new mechanism for capturing geographic knowledge. A GIS is a system for management, analysis, and display of geographic knowledge, which is represented using a series of information sets. These information sets include the following:

Maps and globes

Maps and globes contain interactive views of geographic data with which to answer questions, present results, and use as a dashboard for real work. They provide the advanced GIS applications for interacting with geographic data.

Geographic datasets

Geographic datasets contain file bases and databases of geographic information—features, networks, topologies, terrains, surveys, and attributes.

Data models

GIS datasets are more than database management system (DBMS) tables or individual data files. They incorporate advanced behavior and integrity rules. The schema, behavior, and integrity rules defined in data models play a critical role in GIS.

Processing and work flow models

Collections of geoprocessing procedures that provide tools for analysis and automating and repeating multiple tasks.

Metadata

Metadata contains documents that describe other elements. A metadata catalog enables users to organize, discover, and gain access to shared geographic knowledge.

These five elements, along with comprehensive GIS software logic, form the building blocks for assembling an intelligent GIS. Intelligent GIS makes it possible for users to digitally encapsulate and share geographic knowledge. These elements provide a foundation for addressing many challenges using GIS—for example, improvements in efficiency, informed decision making, science-based planning, resource accounting, evaluation, and communication.

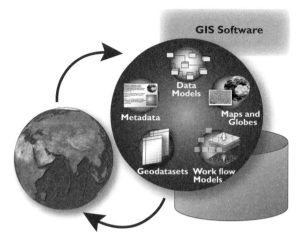

GIS abstracts geography into five basic elements used for representing geographic knowledge. These elements, along with advanced software, provide the building blocks for Intelligent GIS.

Intelligent GIS enables users to capture and share geographic knowledge in many forms—as advanced GIS datasets, maps, data models, standardized work flows, and advanced models of geographic processes. Intelligent GIS also enables the building and management of knowledge repositories that can be published and shared.

GIS must be engineered to enable the creation, use, management, and sharing of all five elements of geographic knowledge.

Geographic information is represented by a series of geographic datasets that model geography using simple, generic data structures. A GIS includes a set of comprehensive tools for working with the geographic data.

A GIS supports several views for working with geographic information:

1. The geodatabase view: A GIS is a spatial database containing datasets that represent geographic information in terms of a generic GIS data model— features, rasters, topologies, networks, and so forth.

2. The geovisualization view: A GIS is a set of intelligent maps and other views that show features and feature relationships on the earth's surface. Various map views of the underlying geographic information can be constructed and used as 'windows into the database' to support queries, analysis, and editing of the information.

3. The geoprocessing view: A GIS is a set of information transformation tools that derive new geographic datasets from existing datasets. These geoprocessing functions take information from existing datasets, apply analytic functions, and write results into newly derived datasets.

These three GIS views are represented in ESRI® ArcGIS® by the catalog (a GIS is a collection of geographic datasets), the map (a GIS is an intelligent map view), and the toolbox (a GIS is a set of geoprocessing tools). Together, all three are critical parts of a complete GIS and are used at varying levels in all GIS applications.

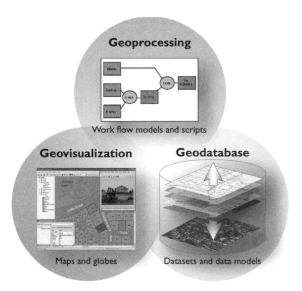

Three views of a GIS for working with key elements of geographic information. All elements can be described, documented, and shared through metadata.

A GIS is a unique kind of database of the world—a geographic database (geodatabase). It is an information system for geography. Fundamentally, a GIS is based on a structured database that describes the world in geographic terms.

Here is a quick review of some key principles that are important in geodatabases.

GEOGRAPHIC REPRESENTATIONS

As part of a GIS geodatabase design, users specify how certain features will be represented. For example, parcels will typically be represented as polygons, streets will be mapped as centerlines, wells as points, and so on. These feature representations are organized into datasets, such as feature classes, raster datasets, and tables.

Each GIS dataset provides a geographic representation of some aspect of the world, including:

- Ordered collections of vector-based features (sets of points, lines, and polygons)

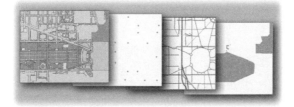

- Raster datasets such as digital elevation models and imagery

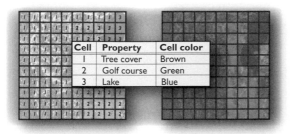

Cell	Property	Cell color
1	Tree cover	Brown
2	Golf course	Green
3	Lake	Blue

- Networks

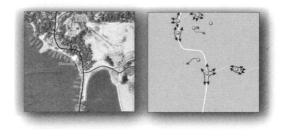

- Terrains and other surfaces

- Survey measurements

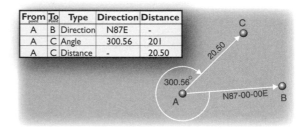

From point	To point	Type	Direction	Distance
A	B	Direction	N87E	-
A	C	Angle	300.56	201
A	C	Distance	-	20.50

- Other data types, such as addresses, place names, and cartographic information

Addresses
3350 45th Ave NE
3383 30th Ave NE
2459 Country Rd. 9 NE

DESCRIPTIVE ATTRIBUTES

In addition to geographic representations, GIS datasets include traditional tabular attributes that describe the geographic objects. Many tables can be linked to the geographic objects by a common thread of fields, or keys. Tables and relationships play a key role in GIS data models, just as they do in traditional database applications.

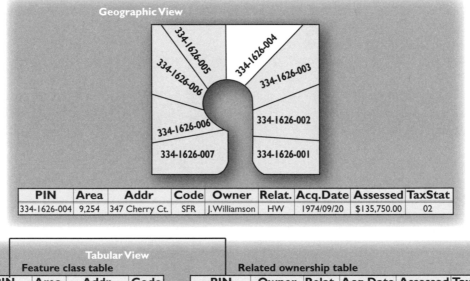

Relationships between features and descriptive attributes

SPATIAL RELATIONSHIPS: TOPOLOGY AND NETWORKS

Spatial relationships, such as topologies and networks, are also crucial parts of a GIS database. Topology is employed to manage common boundaries between features, define and enforce data integrity rules, and support topological queries and navigation—for example, to determine feature adjacency and connectivity. Topology is also used to support sophisticated editing and to construct features from unstructured geometry—for example, to construct polygons from lines.

Networks describe a connected graph of GIS objects that can be traversed. This is important for modeling pathways and navigation for transportation, pipelines, utilities, hydrology, and many other network-based applications.

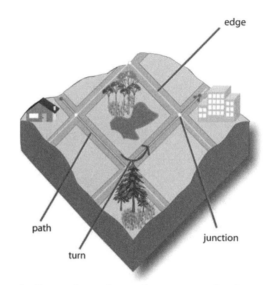

In this network example, street features represent edges that connect at their endpoints (junctions) and are used to model the movement from one edge to another.

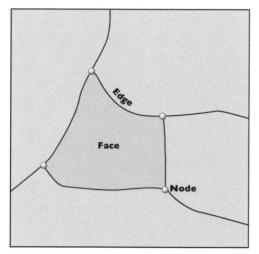

Geographic features share geometry. Feature geometry can be described using relationships between nodes, edges, and faces.

THEMATIC LAYERS AND DATASETS

GIS organizes geographic data into a series of thematic layers and tables. Since geographic datasets in a GIS are georeferenced, they have real-world locations and overlay one another.

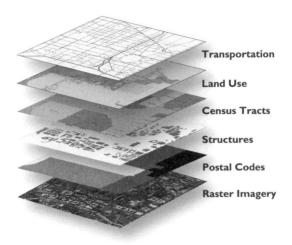

Transportation

Land Use

Census Tracts

Structures

Postal Codes

Raster Imagery

GIS integrates many types of spatial data.

In a GIS, homogeneous collections of geographic objects are organized into layers, such as parcels, wells, buildings, orthophoto imagery, and raster-based digital elevation models (DEMs). Each layer is georeferenced to specific locations. Precisely defined geographic datasets are critical for a useful GIS, and the layer-based concept of thematic collections of information is a critical GIS dataset concept.

Datasets can represent:

• Raw measurements such as satellite imagery

• Compiled and interpreted information

• Data that is derived through geoprocessing operations for analysis and modeling

Many of the spatial relationships between layers can be easily derived through their common geographic location.

GIS manages simple data layers as generic GIS object classes and utilizes a rich collection of tools to work with the data layers to derive many key relationships.

A GIS will use numerous datasets with many representations, often from many organizations. Therefore, it is important for GIS datasets to be:

• Simple to use and easy to understand

• Used easily with other geographic datasets

• Effectively compiled and validated

• Clearly documented for content, intended uses, and purposes

Any GIS database or file base will adhere to these common principles and concepts. Each GIS requires a mechanism for describing geographic data in these terms, along with a comprehensive set of tools to use and manage this information.

Another key aspect of a GIS is the ability to create and work with intelligent maps and other views of geographic information. Interactive and printed maps, three-dimensional (3D) scenes and globes, summary charts and tables, time-based views, and schematic views of network relationships are examples of how GIS users interact with geographic information.

Maps provide a powerful metaphor to define and standardize how people use and interact with their geographic datasets. Interactive maps provide the main user interface for most GIS applications. Users can point to locations and discover new relationships, perform editing and analysis, and effectively present results using geographic views such as maps and globes. ArcMap™ is a key application to create and interact with maps in ArcGIS. With the ArcGIS 3D Analyst™ extension, 3D global views can be created and used.

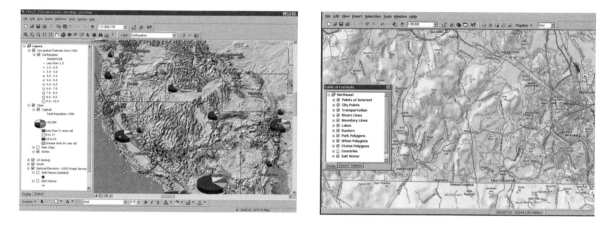

Maps are used to convey geographic information as well as to perform numerous tasks, including advanced data compilation, cartography, analysis, query, and field data collection.

GIS users pan and zoom interactive maps, where map layers apply symbols based on a set of attributes and perform query and analysis operations through the map layers. For example, parcels can be shaded with colors based on their zoning types, or the size of point symbols for oil wells can be specified based on production levels. A GIS user can point to a geographic object in an interactive map to get information about the object. Stores of a certain type can be found within a specified distance of schools, or the wetland areas within 500 meters of selected roads can be identified. In addition, GIS users can edit data and feature representations through interactive maps.

Through an interactive map, GIS users perform the most common GIS tasks from simple to advanced. It's the main 'business form' in a GIS that enables access to geographic information for an organization.

Developers often embed maps in custom applications, and many users publish Web maps on the Internet for focused GIS use.

In addition to maps, other interactive views, such as temporal, globe, and schematic drawings, are used as views into GIS databases.

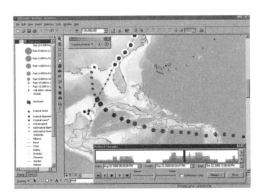

Temporal views used to track hurricanes

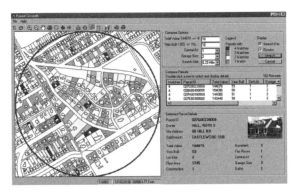

Embedded maps within custom applications

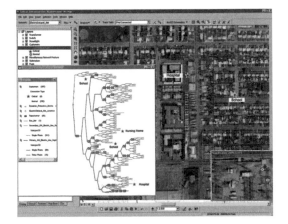

Schematics drawing used to display gas lines

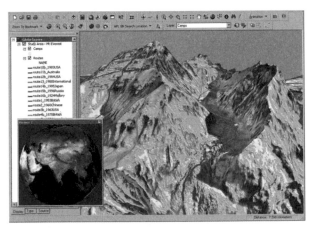

ArcGlobe used to depict Mt. Everest climbing routes

Time-based information (that can be recorded as events) in the ArcGIS Tracking Analyst extension; an example of ArcGIS Schematics, an extension that uses the MapControl for parcel searching; and a view within ArcGlobe.

Geographic datasets can represent raw measurements (for example, satellite imagery), information interpreted and compiled by analysts (for example, roads, buildings, and soil types), or information derived from other data sources using analysis and modeling algorithms. Geoprocessing refers to the tools and processes used to generate derived datasets.

A GIS includes a rich set of tools to work with and process geographic information. This collection of tools is used to operate on the GIS information objects, such as the datasets, attribute fields, and cartographic elements for printed maps. Together, these comprehensive tools and the data objects on which they operate form the basis of a rich geoprocessing framework.

DATA + TOOL = NEW DATA

GIS tools are the building blocks for assembling multistep operations. A tool applies an operation to existing data to derive new data. The geoprocessing framework in a GIS is used to string together a series of these operations, enabling users to automate work flows, program analytical models, and build recurring procedures.

Stringing a sequence of operations together forms a process model that is used to automate and record numerous geoprocessing tasks in the GIS. The building and application of such procedures is referred to as geoprocessing.

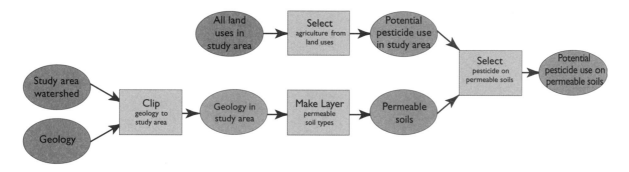

A complete GIS contains generic information and a rich set of GIS operators to work with the information. ArcGIS has a rich GIS language with thousands of operators that work on all the various geographic data types in a GIS.

GEOPROCESSING IN ACTION

Geoprocessing is used in virtually all phases of a GIS for data automation and compilation, data management, analysis and modeling, and advanced cartography.

Geoprocessing is used to model how data flows from one structure to another to perform many common GIS tasks—for example, to import data from numerous formats, integrate that data into the GIS, and perform a number of standard-quality validation checks against the imported data, as well as perform powerful analysis and modeling. The ability to automate and repeat such work flows is a key capability in a GIS. It is widely applied in numerous GIS applications and scenarios.

One method used to build geoprocessing work flows is to execute a number of tools in a specific sequence. Users can compose such processes graphically using the ModelBuilder™ application in ArcGIS, and they can compose scripts using modern scripting tools, such as Python, VBScript, and JavaScript.

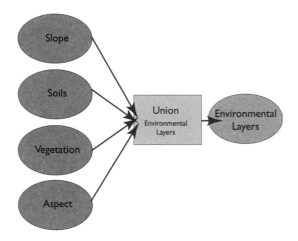

A GIS includes a set of tools and data types that can be assembled into processes in a geoprocessing framework. Many multistep geoprocessing operations can be authored, executed, and shared in ArcGIS.

DATA COMPILATION

Data compilation procedures are automated using geoprocessing to ensure data quality and integrity and to perform repetitive quality assurance/quality control (QA/QC) tasks. Automating these work flows using geoprocessing helps to share and communicate the series of procedures, perform batch processing flows, and document these key processes for derived data.

ANALYSIS AND MODELING

Geoprocessing is the key framework for modeling and analysis. Some common modeling applications include:

- Models for suitability and capability, prediction, and assessment of alternative scenarios

- Integration of external models

- Model sharing

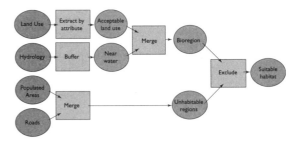

Models can be shared within an organization

DATA MANAGEMENT

Managing GIS data flows is critical in all GIS applications. GIS users apply geoprocessing functions to move data in and out of databases; publish data in many formats, such as in Geography Markup Language (GML) profiles; join adjacent datasets; update GIS database schemas; and perform batch processes on their GIS databases.

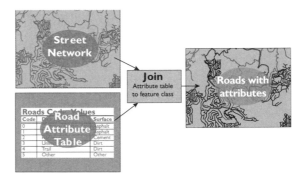

Creating new data by combining existing data

CARTOGRAPHY

Advanced geoprocessing tools are used to derive multiscale cartographic representations, perform generalization logic, and automate much of the cartographic QA/QC work flows for print-quality map products.

GIS information management shares many of the same concepts and characteristics with standard information technology (IT) architectures and can work well in centralized, enterprise computing environments. For example, GIS datasets can be managed in relational databases, just like other enterprise information. Advanced application logic is used to operate on the data stored in the DBMS. Like other transactional enterprise information, GIS systems are used to manage constant change and updates in geographic databases. However, a GIS differs in a number of critical aspects.

GIS DATA IS COMPLEX

GIS data volumes are quite large in the number and size of elements. For example, a simple database query to populate a common business form delivers a few rows of data from the DBMS, while a map draw will require a database query that returns hundreds, even thousands of records. In addition, the vector or raster geometry being retrieved for display can be several megabytes and larger in size for each record. GIS data also has complex relationships and structures, such as networks, terrains, and topologies.

GIS DATA COMPILATION IS AN ADVANCED, SPECIALIZED ACTIVITY

Comprehensive editing applications are required to graphically build and maintain GIS datasets. Specialized processing, along with geographic rules and commands, are necessary to maintain the integrity and behavior of geographic features and rasters. Hence, GIS data compilation is expensive. This is one of the compelling reasons why users often share GIS datasets.

GIS INVOLVES A UNIQUE COMBINATION OF SCIENTIFIC AND BUSINESS COMPUTING

GIS users work with numerous datasets in many formats and data structures simultaneously. In addition to dataset compilation, users constantly produce new result sets and generate model results, maps, globes, layers, and reports. Many of these can be shared and used more than once, while other results are reserved for personal use.

A complete GIS includes management tools to organize and manage the information collections resulting from these work flows. In addition, the GIS must also provide a means for cataloging and sharing this information.

A GIS IS TRANSACTIONAL

As in other DBMSs, numerous data updates are constantly being posted to a GIS database. Hence, GIS databases, like other databases, must support update transactions. However, GIS users have some specialized transactional requirements. The main concept underlying this is often referred to as a long transaction.

In a GIS, a single editing operation can involve changes to multiple rows in multiple tables. Users need to be able to undo and redo their changes before they are committed. Editing sessions can span a few hours or even days. Often the edits must be performed in a system that is disconnected from the central, shared database.

In many cases, database updates pass through a series of phases. For example, within the utilities industry, common work stages include working, proposed, accepted, under construction, and as built. The process is essentially cyclical. The work order is initially generated, assigned to an engineer, and modified over time as it progresses from stage to stage. Finally, the changes are committed, or applied back to the corporate database.

GIS work flow processes may span days and months. Yet the GIS database still requires continuous availability for daily operations for which users might have their own views or states of the shared GIS database.

Examples of other GIS data work flows include:

- Disconnected editing: Some users need the ability to check out portions of the GIS database and replicate it at another location in an independent, standalone system. For example, for field editing, a user could tear off some data, take it into the field to perform edits and updates, then post the changes to the main database.

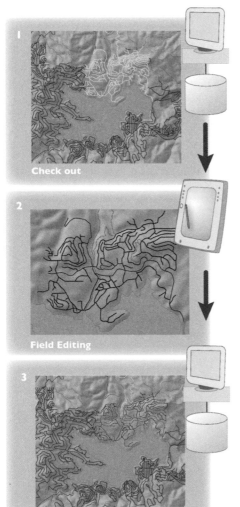

Work stages for disconnected editing on a remote workstation

- Distributed geographic databases: A regional database may be a partial copy for a particular geographic region of the main corporate GIS database. Periodically, the databases must be synchronized by exchanging updates between them.

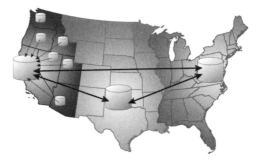

Distributed geodatabases that exchange updates

- Loosely coupled replication across the DBMS: Often, users want to synchronize GIS data contents among a series of database copies (called replicas), where each site performs its own updates on its local database. Periodically, the users want to transfer the updates from each database replica to the others and synchronize their contents. Many times, the DBMSs are different—for example, SQL Server™, Oracle®, and IBM® DB2®.

Today, there is widespread recognition that the data layers and tables in most geographic information systems come from multiple organizations. Each GIS organization develops some, but not all, of its data content. At least some of the layers come from outside the organization. The need for data drives users to acquire their data in the most effective and timely manner, including acquiring portions of their GIS databases from other GIS users.

Thus, GIS data management is distributed among many users.

INTEROPERABILITY

The distributed nature of GIS has many implications for interoperability between multiple GIS organizations and systems. Collaboration among GIS users is crucial.

GIS users have long relied on collaborative efforts for data sharing and use. Recent trends and efforts on GIS standards reflect this fundamental need. Adherence to industry standards and commonly adopted GIS practices is critical to the success of any GIS. A GIS must support critical standards and be able to adapt and evolve support as new standards emerge.

GIS NETWORKS

Many geographic datasets can be compiled and managed as a generic information resource and shared among a community of users. In addition, GIS users have envisioned how sharing these commonly used datasets can be accomplished through the Web.

Web nodes, or GIS catalog portals, can be implemented to allow GIS users to register, as well as discover, geographic information for access and use. As a consequence, GIS technology is becoming increasingly connected on the Web for information sharing and use.

This vision has been in existence for more than a decade, and it has been described as a National Spatial Data Infrastructure (NSDI) or a Global Spatial Data Infrastructure (GSDI). These concepts are in general use today, not only at national and global levels, but also within states and local communities. This concept is collectively referred to as a Spatial Data Infrastructure (SDI).

A GIS network is an implementation of an SDI. It is a federation of user sites that discover, use, and publish shared geographic information on the Web.

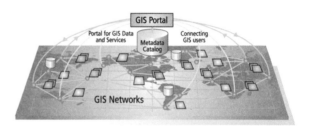

Geographic intelligence is inherently distributed and loosely integrated. Rarely is all the necessary information present in a single database instance with a single data schema. GIS users count on one another for portions of their GIS data. GIS networks enable users to connect to one another and share their geographic knowledge.

A GIS network has three key building blocks:

- Metadata catalog portals, where users can search for and discover GIS information relevant to their needs

- GIS nodes, where users compile and publish GIS information sets

- GIS users who search for, discover, and connect to and use published GIS data and services

The three key building blocks in a GIS network

GIS CATALOG PORTALS

An important component in any GIS network is a GIS catalog portal with a registry of the numerous data holdings and information sets. A number of GIS users act as data stewards who compile and publish their datasets for shared use by other organizations. They register their information sets at a catalog portal. By searching a catalog portal, other GIS users can find and connect to desired information sets.

The GIS catalog portal is a Web site where GIS users can search for and find GIS information relevant to their needs and, as such, depends on a network of published GIS services for sharing maps, datasets, metadata catalogs, geoprocessing, and data management services. Periodically, a GIS catalog portal site can harvest catalogs from a collection of participating sites to publish one central GIS

catalog. Thus, a GIS catalog can reference data holdings contained at its site as well as at other sites. It is envisioned that a series of catalog nodes will be available to form a network—an SDI.

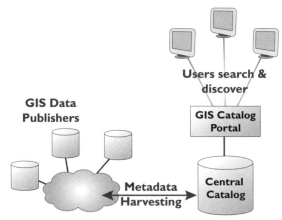

GIS data and services are documented in catalog records in a GIS catalog portal that can be searched to find candidates for use in various GIS applications.

One example of a GIS catalog portal is the U.S. government's Geospatial One-Stop portal (www.geodata.gov). This portal makes it easier, faster, and less expensive for all levels of government and the public to access geographic information.

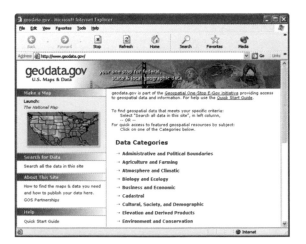

geodata.gov is a node in the United States' National Spatial Data Infrastructure.

GIS requirements influence how ArcGIS is built and used. GIS, like other information technologies, must be implemented in a manner that easily allows applications to support each organization's work flows and business requirements. This is accomplished by providing a generic software platform that supports a variety of geographic dataset types as well as comprehensive tools for data management, editing, analysis, and display.

In this context, ArcGIS can be increasingly thought of as IT infrastructure for assembling large, sophisticated, multiuser systems. A GIS platform must provide all the capabilities necessary to support this enlarged vision:

- A geographic database to store and manage all geographic objects

- A Web-based network for distributed geographic information management and sharing

- Desktop and server applications for:

  o Data compilation

  o Information queries

  o Spatial analysis and geoprocessing

  o Cartographic production

  o Image visualization and exploitation

  o GIS data management

- Modular software components (engines) to embed GIS logic in other applications and to build custom applications

- Geographic information services for enterprise and federated GIS systems

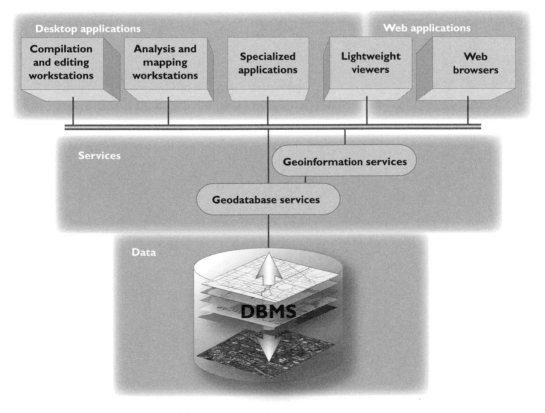

A comprehensive GIS platform designed to facilitate geographic requirements

2 What is ArcGIS?

In the early decades of GIS, professionals concentrated primarily on data compilation and focused application projects, spending a majority of their time creating GIS databases and authoring geographic knowledge. Gradually, GIS professionals began to use and exploit these knowledge collections in numerous GIS applications and settings. Users applied comprehensive GIS workstations to compile geographic datasets, build work flows for data compilation and quality control, author maps and analytical models, and document their work and methods.

This reinforced the traditional view of a GIS user with a professional scientific workstation that connects to datasets and databases. The workstation had a comprehensive GIS application with advanced GIS logic and tools that were used to accomplish almost any GIS task.

This concept of a GIS software seat has proven invaluable and is widely adopted by GIS professionals in nearly 200,000 organizations worldwide. In fact, this client/server computing model has been so successful that many only think of GIS within this context. However, the GIS vision is expanding.

Recent developments in computing—the growth of the Internet, advances in DBMS technology, object-oriented programming, mobile computing, and widespread GIS adoption—have led to an evolving vision and role for GIS. The vision of a GIS platform is expanding.

In addition to GIS desktops, GIS software can be centralized in application servers and Web servers to deliver GIS capabilities to any number of users over networks. Focused sets of GIS logic can be embedded and deployed in custom applications. And increasingly, GIS is deployed in mobile devices for field GIS.

Enterprise GIS users connect to central GIS servers using traditional, advanced GIS desktops as well as Web browsers, focused applications, mobile computing devices, and digital appliances.

The ArcGIS product line was built to satisfy these evolving requirements to deliver a scalable, comprehensive GIS platform, as illustrated in the diagram below.

ArcGIS

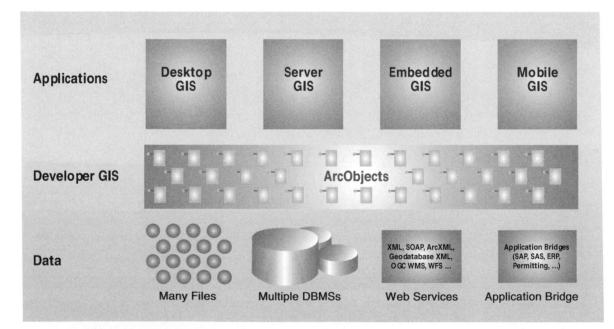

ArcGIS is a complete GIS software system.

ArcGIS provides a scalable framework for implementing GIS for a single user or many users on desktops, in servers, over the Web, and in the field. ArcGIS is an integrated collection of GIS software products for building a complete GIS. It consists of a number of frameworks for deploying GIS:

- ArcGIS Desktop—An integrated suite of professional GIS applications

- ArcGIS Engine—Embeddable developer components for building custom GIS applications

- Server GIS—ArcSDE®, ArcIMS®, and ArcGIS Server

- Mobile GIS—ArcPad® as well as ArcGIS Desktop and ArcGIS Engine for Tablet PC computing

ArcGIS is based on ArcObjects™, a common, modular library of shared GIS software components.

ArcObjects includes a wide variety of programmable components, ranging from fine-grained objects (for example, individual geometry objects) to coarse-grained objects (for example, a map object to interact with existing ArcMap documents), which aggregate comprehensive GIS functionality for developers. Each of the ArcGIS product architectures built with ArcObjects represents alternative application development platforms for GIS software developers, including desktop GIS (ArcGIS Desktop), embedded GIS (ArcGIS Engine), and server GIS (ArcGIS Server).

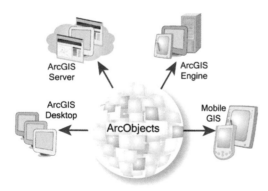

ArcObjects—The developer building blocks for ArcGIS

DESKTOP GIS

Desktop GIS is the primary seat from which GIS professionals compile, author, and use geographic information and knowledge. GIS professionals use a standard desktop as a productivity tool for authoring, sharing, managing, and publishing geographic knowledge.

ArcGIS Desktop is an integrated suite of advanced GIS applications. It includes a series of Windows®-based desktop applications—ArcMap, ArcCatalog™, ArcToolbox™, and ArcGlobe™—with user interface components. ArcGIS Desktop is available at three functional levels—ArcView®, ArcEditor™, and ArcInfo®—and can be customized and extended using the ArcGIS Desktop Developer Kit, which is included.

For more information about ArcGIS Desktop, see Chapter 3, 'Desktop GIS: ArcView, ArcEditor, and ArcInfo'.

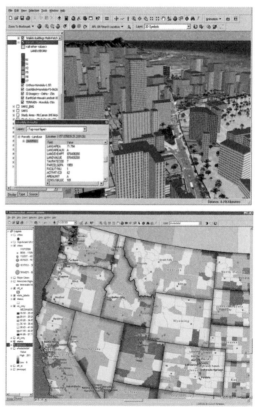

The graphics above represent applications using ArcGIS Desktop

SERVER GIS

GIS users deploy a centralized server GIS to publish and share geographic knowledge within large organizations and with many other users on the Internet. Server GIS software is used for any kind of centrally hosted GIS computing, including support for GIS data management and geoprocessing. In addition to serving maps and data, a GIS server can provide all the functionality of a GIS workstation in a shared central server, including mapping, spatial analysis, complex spatial queries, advanced data compilation, distributed data management, batch geoprocessing, enforcement of geometric integrity rules, and so on.

GIS servers are IT-compliant and work well with other enterprise software, such as Web servers, DBMSs, and enterprise frameworks including .NET and Java™ 2 Platform Enterprise Edition (J2EE). This enables the integration of GIS with numerous other information system technologies.

ArcGIS includes three server products

ArcSDE—An advanced spatial data server for managing geographic information in numerous relational database management systems (RDBMSs). ArcSDE is the data server between ArcGIS and relational databases. It is widely used to enable geodatabases to be shared by many users across any network and to scale in size to any level necessary.

ArcIMS—A scalable Internet map server for GIS publishing of maps, data, and metadata through open Internet protocols. ArcIMS is already deployed in tens of thousands of organizations and is used primarily for GIS Web publishing—delivering data and map services to many users on the Web.

ArcGIS Server—An application server that includes a shared library of GIS software objects to build server-side GIS applications in enterprise and Web computing frameworks. ArcGIS Server is used for building central enterprise GIS applications, Simple Object Access Protocol (SOAP)-based Web services, and Web applications.

For more information about the ArcGIS server products, see Chapter 4, 'Server GIS: ArcSDE, ArcIMS, and ArcGIS Server'.

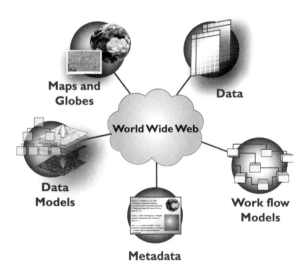

Emerging Internet technology, such as Web services, holds great promise for GIS users to share and serve geographic knowledge and to connect GIS across organizations.

DEVELOPER GIS

The ESRI Developer Network (EDN) is a developer product that provides a comprehensive system for developing applications with ArcGIS. EDN provides a unified programming environment and tools that enable developers to:

- Embed GIS and mapping functionality in other applications.

- Build and deploy custom ArcGIS Desktop applications.

- Configure and customize ArcGIS products, such as ArcView, ArcEditor, and ArcInfo.

- Extend the ArcGIS architecture and data model.

- Build Web services and server-based applications.

EDN includes all the developer resources of ArcGIS Desktop, ArcGIS Server, ArcIMS, ArcSDE, and the embeddable components of ArcGIS Engine.

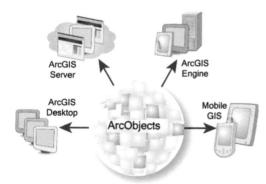

The core of the EDN Developer Kit is a common library of software components, ArcObjects, that programmers can use to embed and extend GIS using standard programming environments such as C++, .NET, and Java.

For more information about Developer GIS, see Chapter 6, 'ESRI Developer Network'.

ArcGIS Engine

Embedded GIS can add selected GIS components to focused applications to deliver GIS functionality anywhere in an organization. This enables access to GIS functions through simple, focused interfaces by many who need to apply GIS as a tool in their daily work. For example, embedded GIS applications support remote data collection, custom interfaces for operators, and focused data compilation activities, as well as allow GIS use by managers and end users.

ArcGIS Engine provides a series of embeddable user interface components—for example, a Map Control and a Globe Control that can be used to embed interactive maps or globes in any application. With ArcGIS Engine, developers can build focused GIS solutions with simple interfaces to access any set of GIS functions using C++, Component Object Model (COM), .NET, or Java.

Developers can build complete custom applications with ArcGIS Engine or embed GIS logic in existing user applications—for example, Microsoft® Word or Excel—to deploy custom GIS applications that deliver focused GIS solutions to many users.

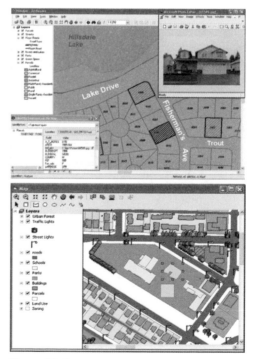

Use ArcGIS Engine to embed GIS into your applications.

MOBILE GIS

Increasingly, GIS is moving from the office into the field by means of focused application solutions on mobile computing devices. Wireless mobile devices enabled with global positioning systems (GPS) are increasingly used for focused data collection and GIS information access in the field. Firefighters, waste collectors, engineering crews, surveyors, utility workers, soldiers, census workers, police, and field biologists represent a few types of field workers who use mobile GIS as a tool.

Some field-based tasks require relatively simple geographic tools, and others involve complex operations requiring sophisticated GIS tools. ArcGIS includes applications encompassing both of these needs. ArcPad is the ArcGIS solution for mobile GIS and field computing, such as incident reporting of spatially recorded accidents. These types of tasks are typically performed on handheld computers (running Microsoft Windows CE or Pocket PC). ArcGIS Desktop and ArcGIS Engine focus on field tasks that require GIS analysis and decision making. These tasks are typically performed on high-end Tablet PCs.

For more information about mobile GIS, see Chapter 7, 'Mobile GIS using ArcPad and ArcGIS'.

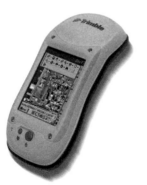

You can use ArcPad to take GIS into the field.

THE GEODATABASE

The geodatabase—short for geographic database—is the core geographic information model used to organize GIS data into thematic layers and spatial representations.

The geodatabase is a comprehensive series of application logic and tools for accessing and managing GIS data. The geodatabase application logic is accessible in client applications (ArcGIS Desktop), server configurations (ArcGIS Server), and logic embedded in custom applications (ArcGIS Engine).

The geodatabase is a GIS and DBMS standards-based physical data store and is implemented on a number of multiuser and personal DBMSs and in XML.

Geodatabase application logic is used to work with datasets in hundreds of formats and data structures, and it is also used to implement advanced GIS data objects, such as topologies, networks, raster catalogs, relationships, and domains.

The geodatabase was designed as an open, simple geometry storage model. Open to many possible storage mechanisms, including DBMS files and XML implementations, the geodatabase is not tied to a single DBMS vendor.

For more information about the geodatabase, see Chapter 8, 'GIS data concepts and the geodatabase'.

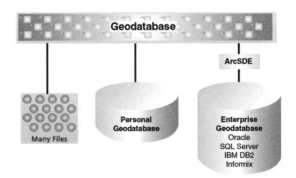

Geodatabase application logic is used to work with all geographic data in ArcGIS and adds rich GIS behavior to simple data structures.

3

Desktop GIS: ArcView, ArcEditor, and ArcInfo

ArcGIS Desktop includes a suite of integrated applications including ArcCatalog, ArcMap, ArcGlobe, ArcToolbox, and ModelBuilder. Using these applications and interfaces in unison, users can perform any GIS task, from simple to advanced, including mapping, geographic analysis, data editing and compilation, data management, visualization, and geoprocessing.

ArcGIS Desktop is scalable and can address the needs of many types of users. It is available at three functional levels:

1. **ArcView** focuses on comprehensive data use, mapping, and analysis.

2. **ArcEditor** adds advanced geographic editing and data creation.

3. **ArcInfo** is a complete, professional GIS desktop containing comprehensive GIS functionality, including rich geoprocessing tools.

Additional capabilities can be added to all seats through a series of ArcGIS Desktop extension products from ESRI and other organizations. Users can also develop their own custom extensions to ArcGIS Desktop by working with ArcObjects, the ArcGIS software component library. Users develop extensions and custom tools using standard Windows programming interfaces such as Visual Basic® (VB), .NET, and Visual C++®.

ArcGIS Desktop contains complete GIS capabilities and support for the following:
Mapping and 3D visualization
Raster and vector editing
Geoprocessing
Geographic data management in a comprehensive information model and framework • Datasets • Topology, integrity rules, and rich GIS behavior • Maps and globes • Geoprocessing tools, models, and work flows • Metadata, catalog, and database management
Data interoperability (to work with unlimited files, formats, and data sizes)
Maintaining and sharing data updates and work flows in a transaction model
GIS interoperability standards such as Open Geospatial Consortium (OGC) and International Organization for Standardization (ISO)
Web services • Map publishing • Data publishing and delivery • Editing • Geoprocessing

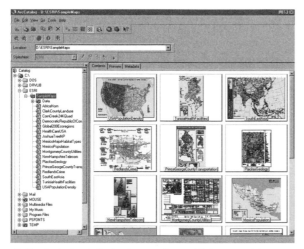

ArcCatalog is the application for managing spatial datasets and data models as well as for recording, viewing, and managing metadata.

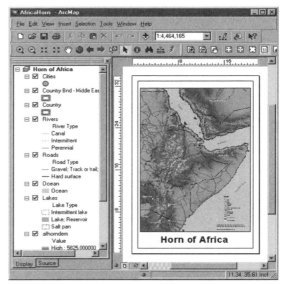

ArcMap is used for all mapping and editing tasks as well as map-based analysis.

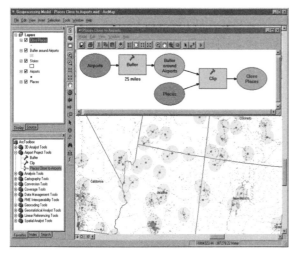

ArcToolbox and ModelBuilder are used for geoprocessing and spatial analysis.

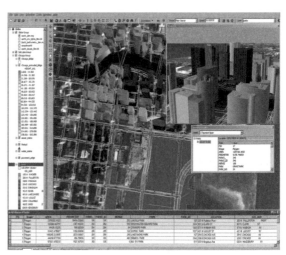

ArcGlobe, an application included with the ArcGIS 3D Analyst extension, provides an interactive global view to work with geographic data.

ArcMap

ArcMap is the central application in ArcGIS Desktop for all map-based tasks including cartography, map analysis, and editing. ArcMap is a comprehensive map authoring application for ArcGIS Desktop.

ArcMap offers two types of map views: a geographic data view and a page layout view. In the geographic data view, users work with geographic layers to symbolize, analyze, and compile GIS datasets. A table of contents interface helps organize and control the drawing properties of the GIS data layers in the data frame. The data view is a window into any GIS dataset for a given area.

In the layout view, users work with map pages that contain geographic data views as well as other map elements, such as scalebars, legends, North arrows, and reference maps. ArcMap is used to compose maps on pages for printing and publishing.

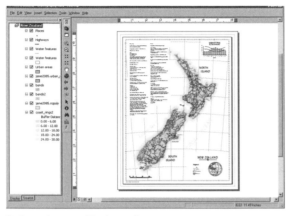

Design and create publication-quality maps.

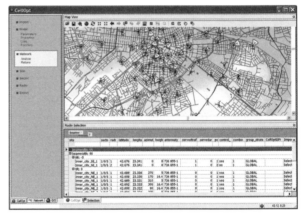

Author and share maps with ArcReader, ArcGIS Engine, ArcIMS, and ArcGIS Server.

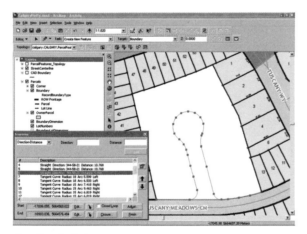

Compile and edit data.

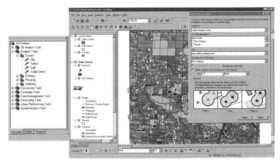

Perform modeling and analysis.

ARCCATALOG

The ArcCatalog application helps users organize and manage all geographic information, such as maps, globes, datasets, models, metadata, and services. It includes tools to:

- Browse and find geographic information.

- Record, view, and manage metadata.

- Define, export, and import geodatabase data models.

- Search for and discover GIS data on local networks and the Web.

- Administer a GIS server.

Users can employ ArcCatalog to find, organize, and use GIS data as well as to document data holdings using standards-based metadata.

A GIS database administrator uses ArcCatalog to define and build geodatabases. A GIS server administrator uses ArcCatalog to administer the GIS server framework.

Metadata in ArcCatalog

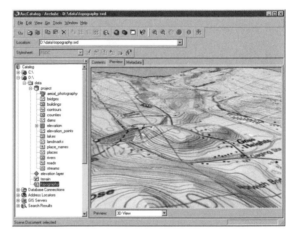

Previewing a 3D scene in ArcCatalog

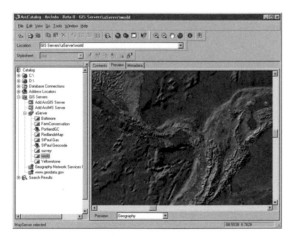

Previewing a map produced with ArcGIS Server in ArcCatalog

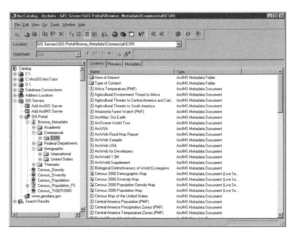

Organizing, editing, and managing a metadata catalog in an ArcIMS metadata server

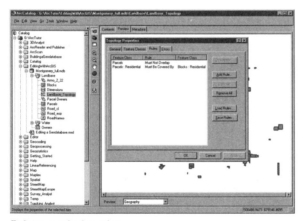

Geoprocessing in ArcCatalog

Defining a geodatabase schema

GEOPROCESSING WITH ArcToolbox AND ModelBuilder

ArcGIS Desktop provides a geoprocessing framework of tools that can be run in several different ways, including through dialog boxes in ArcToolbox, as inputs to models in ModelBuilder, as commands in the command line, and as functions in scripts. This framework facilitates the creation, use, documentation, and sharing of geoprocessing models. The two main parts of the geoprocessing framework include ArcToolbox, an organized collection of geoprocessing tools, and ModelBuilder, a visual modeling language for building geoprocessing work flows and scripts.

ArcToolbox

ArcToolbox contains a comprehensive collection of geoprocessing functions, including tools for:

- Data management

- Data conversion

- Coverage processing

- Vector analysis

- Geocoding

- Linear referencing

- Cartography

- Statistical analysis

ArcToolbox is embedded in ArcCatalog and ArcMap and is available in ArcView, ArcEditor, and ArcInfo.

Each product level includes additional geoprocessing tools:

- ArcView supports a core set of simple data loading and translation tools as well as fundamental analysis tools.

- ArcEditor adds a number of tools for geodatabase creation, loading, and schema management.

- ArcInfo provides a comprehensive set of tools for vector analysis, data conversion, data loading, and coverage geoprocessing.

Although geoprocessing is accessible in ArcView and ArcEditor, ArcInfo is the primary geoprocessing seat in a GIS organization because it contains comprehensive geoprocessing tools for performing significant GIS analysis. At least one ArcInfo seat is needed to build GIS data and perform analysis.

Additional geoprocessing toolsets come with many of the ArcGIS extensions, such as ArcGIS Spatial Analyst, which includes up to 200 raster modeling tools, and ArcGIS 3D Analyst, which includes many triangulated irregular network (TIN) and terrain analysis tools. ArcGIS Network Analyst includes a number of transportation and network tools. ArcGIS Geostatistical Analyst adds kriging and surface interpolation tools.

ArcToolbox is available in all ArcGIS Desktop applications such as ArcCatalog.

ModelBuilder

The ModelBuilder interface provides a graphical modeling framework for designing and implementing geoprocessing models that can include tools, scripts, and data. Models are data flow diagrams that string together a series of tools and data to create advanced procedures and work flows.

Users can drag tools and datasets onto a model and connect them to create an ordered sequence of steps to perform complex GIS tasks.

ModelBuilder is a productive mechanism to share methods and procedures with others within, as well as outside, an organization.

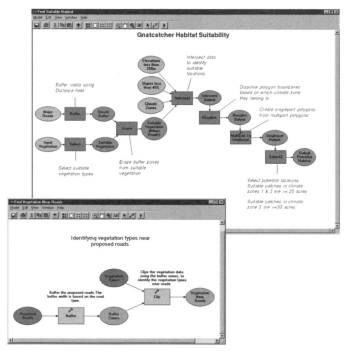

ModelBuilder provides an interactive mechanism for building and executing complex GIS procedures.

ArcGlobe

ArcGlobe, part of the ArcGIS 3D Analyst extension, provides continuous, multiresolution, interactive viewing of geographic information. Like ArcMap, ArcGlobe works with GIS data layers, displaying information in a geodatabase and in all supported GIS data formats. ArcGlobe has a dynamic 3D view of geographic information. ArcGlobe layers are placed within a single global context, integrating all GIS data sources into a common global framework. It handles multiple data resolutions by making datasets visible at appropriate scales and levels of detail.

The ArcGlobe interactive view of geographic information significantly enhances GIS users' ability to integrate and use disparate GIS datasets. It is expected that ArcGlobe will become a widely adopted application platform of choice for common GIS work, such as editing, spatial data analysis, mapping, and visualization.

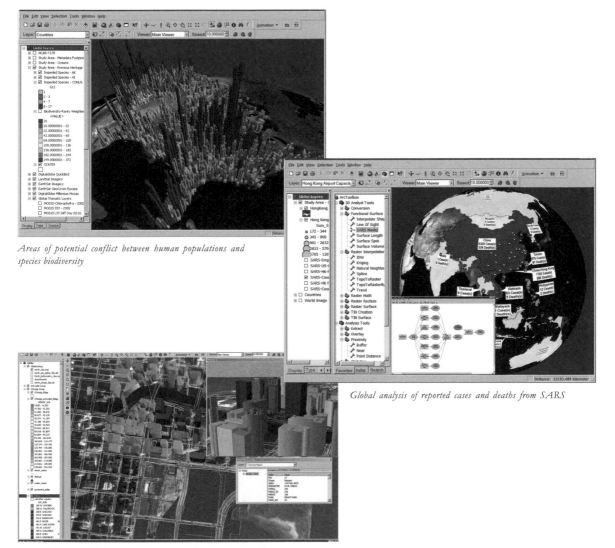

Areas of potential conflict between human populations and species biodiversity

Global analysis of reported cases and deaths from SARS

View of downtown Chicago

WHAT ARE ArcView, ArcEditor, AND ArcInfo?

ArcGIS Desktop is the information authoring and usage tool for GIS professionals. It can be purchased as three separate software products, each providing a higher level of functionality.

- ArcView provides comprehensive mapping, data use, and analysis tools along with simple editing and geoprocessing.

- ArcEditor includes advanced editing capabilities for shapefiles and geodatabases in addition to the full functionality of ArcView.

- ArcInfo is the full-function, flagship ArcGIS Desktop product. It extends the functionality of both ArcView and ArcEditor with advanced geoprocessing. It also includes the legacy applications for ArcInfo Workstation (ArcPlot™, ArcEdit™, ARC Macro Language [AML™], and so on).

Because ArcView, ArcEditor, and ArcInfo all share a common architecture, users working with any of these GIS desktops can share their work with other users. Maps, data, symbology, map layers, custom tools and interfaces, reports, metadata, and so on, can be accessed interchangeably in all three products. Users benefit from using a single architecture, minimizing the need to learn and deploy several different architectures.

In addition, maps, data, and metadata created with ArcGIS Desktop can be shared with many users through the use of free ArcReader™ seats, custom ArcGIS Engine applications, and advanced GIS Web services using ArcIMS and ArcGIS Server.

The capabilities of all three levels can be further extended using a series of optional add-on software extensions such as ArcGIS Spatial Analyst and ArcGIS Network Analyst. For more information on the extension software, see 'Optional extensions for ArcGIS Desktop' later in this chapter.

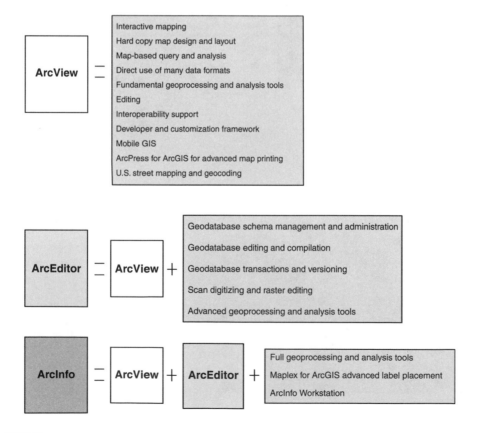

ArcView −
Interactive mapping
Hard copy map design and layout
Map-based query and analysis
Direct use of many data formats
Fundamental geoprocessing and analysis tools
Editing
Interoperability support
Developer and customization framework
Mobile GIS
ArcPress for ArcGIS for advanced map printing
U.S. street mapping and geocoding

ArcEditor − **ArcView** +
Geodatabase schema management and administration
Geodatabase editing and compilation
Geodatabase transactions and versioning
Scan digitizing and raster editing
Advanced geoprocessing and analysis tools

ArcInfo − **ArcView** + **ArcEditor** +
Full geoprocessing and analysis tools
Maplex for ArcGIS advanced label placement
ArcInfo Workstation

WHAT IS ArcView?

ArcView is the first of the three functional product levels of ArcGIS Desktop. ArcView is a suite of applications: ArcMap, ArcCatalog, ArcToolbox, and ModelBuilder. ArcView is a powerful GIS toolkit for data use, mapping, reporting, and map-based analysis.

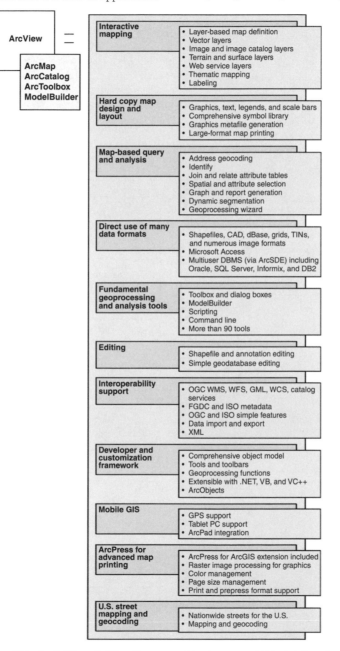

ArcView = **ArcMap** **ArcCatalog** **ArcToolbox** **ModelBuilder**	

Interactive mapping	• Layer-based map definition • Vector layers • Image and image catalog layers • Terrain and surface layers • Web service layers • Thematic mapping • Labeling
Hard copy map design and layout	• Graphics, text, legends, and scale bars • Comprehensive symbol library • Graphics metafile generation • Large-format map printing
Map-based query and analysis	• Address geocoding • Identify • Join and relate attribute tables • Spatial and attribute selection • Graph and report generation • Dynamic segmentation • Geoprocessing wizard
Direct use of many data formats	• Shapefiles, CAD, dBase, grids, TINs, and numerous image formats • Microsoft Access • Multiuser DBMS (via ArcSDE) including Oracle, SQL Server, Informix, and DB2
Fundamental geoprocessing and analysis tools	• Toolbox and dialog boxes • ModelBuilder • Scripting • Command line • More than 90 tools
Editing	• Shapefile and annotation editing • Simple geodatabase editing
Interoperability support	• OGC WMS, WFS, GML, WCS, catalog services • FGDC and ISO metadata • OGC and ISO simple features • Data import and export • XML
Developer and customization framework	• Comprehensive object model • Tools and toolbars • Geoprocessing functions • Extensible with .NET, VB, and VC++ • ArcObjects
Mobile GIS	• GPS support • Tablet PC support • ArcPad integration
ArcPress for advanced map printing	• ArcPress for ArcGIS extension included • Raster image processing for graphics • Color management • Page size management • Print and prepress format support
U.S. street mapping and geocoding	• Nationwide streets for the U.S. • Mapping and geocoding

A list of some of the key capabilities in ArcView. ArcView offers many exciting data use capabilities including advanced map symbology and editing tools, metadata management, and on-the-fly projection.

WHAT IS ArcEditor?

ArcEditor is a GIS data automation and compilation workstation for the construction and maintenance of geodatabases, shapefiles, and other geographic information. ArcEditor, along with ArcInfo, enables GIS users to fully exploit the rich information model, behaviors, and transaction support of the geodatabase.

ArcEditor provides all the capabilities of ArcView, as well as the ability to create geodatabase behaviors, such as topology, domains, and geometric networks. ArcEditor includes tools that support metadata creation, geographic data exploration and analysis, and mapping, and it includes the ArcScan™ for ArcGIS extension.

ArcEditor also includes comprehensive geoprocessing tools for automating data management work flows and performing analysis.

Implementing a DBMS and accessing it via ArcSDE facilitates multiuser geodatabase editing and maintenance with complete version management in ArcEditor. This includes advanced tools for version management—for example, version merging tools to identify and resolve conflicts, perform disconnected editing, and conduct history management.

For more information on ArcSDE, see the section 'What is ArcSDE?' in Chapter 4, 'Server GIS: ArcSDE, ArcIMS, and ArcGIS Server'.

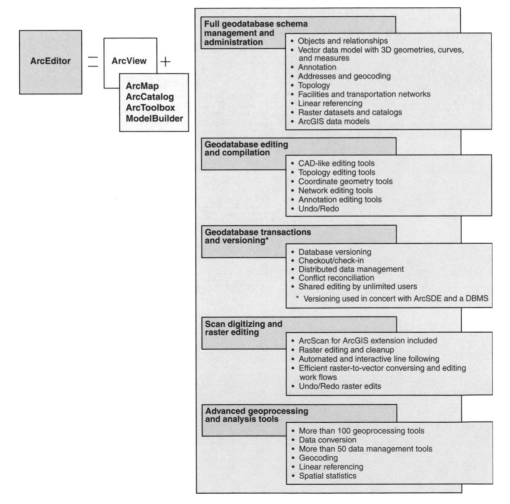

A list of some of the key capabilities of ArcEditor is shown above. ArcEditor offers the same functionality as ArcView but adds advanced editing tools.

WHAT IS ARCINFO?

ArcInfo is the flagship ArcGIS Desktop product. It is the most functionally rich client in ArcGIS Desktop. The high-end ArcInfo product provides all the capabilities of ArcView and ArcEditor. In addition, it includes a comprehensive collection of tools in ArcToolbox to support advanced geoprocessing and polygon processing. The classic workstation applications and capabilities

contained in ArcInfo Workstation, such as Arc, ArcPlot, and ArcEdit, are included as well. By adding advanced geoprocessing, ArcInfo is a complete system for GIS data creation, update, query, mapping, and analysis.

ArcInfo also includes the Maplex for ArcGIS extension.

Any organization requiring a complete GIS needs at least one copy of ArcInfo.

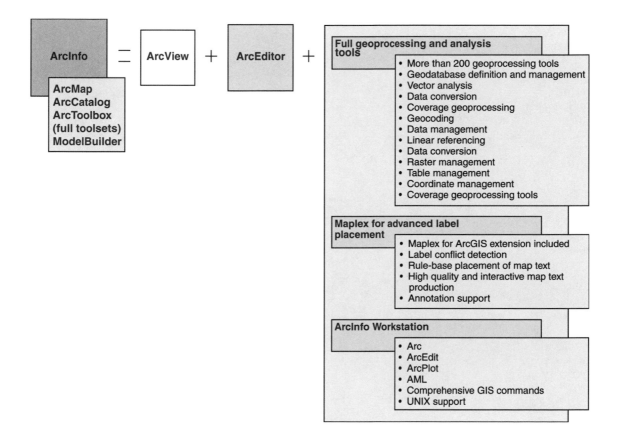

A list of some of the key ArcInfo capabilities is shown above. ArcInfo provides all the capabilities of ArcView and ArcEditor as well as additional geoprocessing functionality. The ArcInfo version of ArcToolbox is important for sites that build and create spatial databases and for advanced analysis.

OPTIONAL EXTENSIONS FOR ArcGIS DESKTOP

Many optional extensions are available for ArcGIS Desktop. Extensions allow users to perform tasks such as raster geoprocessing and three-dimensional analysis. All extensions can be used by each product—ArcView, ArcEditor, and ArcInfo.

The ArcScan for ArcGIS extension is included free of charge with ArcEditor and ArcInfo, and the Maplex for ArcGIS extension is also included with ArcInfo.

ArcGIS 3D Analyst
- ArcGlobe: Interactive 3D scenes
- Globe views in ArcCatalog
- Globe publishing in ArcGIS Publisher
- 3D raster and TIN modeling tools

ArcGIS Business Analyst
- Customer and store prospecting
- Market penetration analysis
- Drive-time analysis

ArcGIS Data Interoperability
- Directly read, transform, and export any data format
- Tools for data transformation and direct use

ArcGIS Geostatistical Analyst
- Advanced kriging and surface modeling
- Exploratory spatial data analysis tools
- Probability, threshold, and error mapping

ArcGIS Network Analyst
- Network and transportation analysis
- Minimum path, closest facility, allocate, and traveling salesman
- Advanced network data modeling and simulation

ArcGIS Publisher
- Publish Map and Globe documents for use with free ArcReader application
- Package and compress data
- Optional data encryption
- Developer SDK for customizing ArcReader

ArcGIS Schematics
- Database-driven schematic rendering and display
- Schematic views of GIS networks and tabular information
- Multiple schematic representations

ArcGIS Spatial Analyst
- Advanced raster and vector tools
- Spatial modeling
- ArcGrid Map Algebra

ArcGIS Survey Analyst
- Comprehensive survey information management using the geodatabase
- Advanced survey computation
- Improved GIS data accuracy via links to survey locations

ArcGIS Tracking Analyst
- Time-based map display and rendering
- Playback tools (play, pause, forward, rewind)
- Work with time-based data (features whose geometry or attributes move and change)

ArcScan for ArcGIS
- Integrated raster-vector editing
- Vectorizing features from raster
- Raster snapping

ArcWeb Services
- Subscriptions to multiple GIS Web services
- Access to rich data and GIS tools
- Plug in, turn on, and use

Maplex for ArcGIS
- Advanced label placement and conflict detection for high-end cartographic production
- Simplifies the labor-intensive placement of map text

ArcGIS 3D Analyst

ArcGIS 3D Analyst enables effective visualization and analysis of surface data. With ArcGIS 3D Analyst, users can view a surface from multiple viewpoints, query a surface, determine what is visible from a chosen location on a surface, and create a realistic perspective image by draping raster and vector data over a surface. The core of the ArcGIS 3D Analyst extension is the ArcGlobe application. ArcGlobe provides the interface for viewing multiple layers of GIS data and for creating and analyzing surfaces.

ArcGIS 3D Analyst also provides advanced GIS tools for three-dimensional modeling such as cut/fill, line of sight, and terrain modeling.

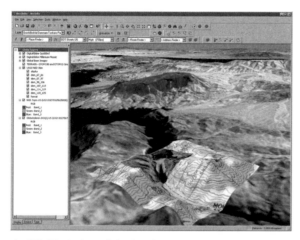

ArcGIS 3D Analyst includes three-dimensional visualization and terrain modeling capabilities.

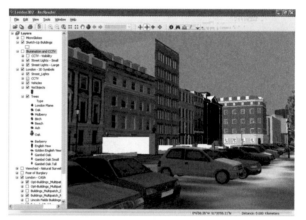

ArcGIS 3D Analyst offers animation tools and functionality.

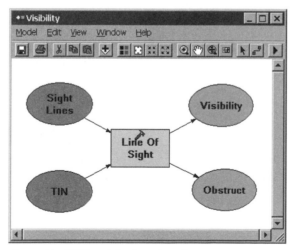

An example of TIN analysis using geoprocessing

ArcGIS Business Analyst

ArcGIS Business Analyst provides advanced analysis tools and a complete data package for analyzing business and demographic information as an aid in making critical business decisions.

ArcGIS Business Analyst includes an extensive collection of business, demographic, and consumer household data and tools for analyzing the market and competition, finding the ideal site for a new business location, or targeting direct mail. ArcGIS Business Analyst lets users perform sophisticated business analysis.

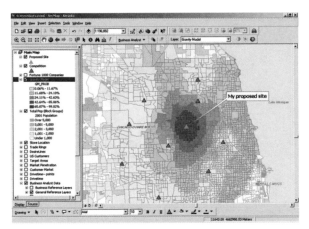

By combining information, such as sales data, demographics, and competitor locations, with geographic data, such as census boundaries, territories, or store locations, ArcGIS Business Analyst helps users better understand their market, customers, and competition.

ArcGIS Business Analyst allows users to:

- Choose site locations.

- Identify and reach potential customers.

- Find new markets.

- Perform customer or store prospecting.

- Define customer-based or store trade areas.

- Identify locations similar to that of their best stores.

- Conduct an analysis of market penetration.

- Create gravity models to forecast potential sales at new stores.

- Perform drive-time analysis over a nationwide street network.

- Search national businesses and add results to any analysis.

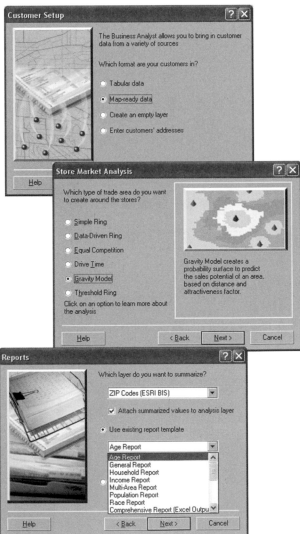

ArcGIS Data Interoperability

The ArcGIS Data Interoperability extension adds the ability to directly read and employ more than 60 common GIS vector data formats, including many of the emerging GML specifications. In addition, GIS data can be delivered in a variety of formats. For example, data sources, such as advanced computer-aided design (CAD) datasets with extended entity attributes, MapInfo® datasets, Intergraph GeoMedia® datasets, and various GML files, can be accessed, displayed, and used directly in ArcGIS. This extension formulates the delivery of GIS data to others in a variety of export vector data formats (more than 50 supported formats).

The ArcGIS Data Interoperability extension also provides a series of data transformation tools to build converters for more complex vector data formats.

The ArcGIS Data Interoperability extension was developed collaboratively by ESRI and Safe Software Inc., the leading GIS interoperability vendor, and is based on Safe Software's popular Feature Manipulation Engine (FME®) product.

With the ArcGIS Data Interoperability extension, users can:

- Add support for many GIS data formats for direct use within ArcGIS, for example, for use in ArcMap, ArcCatalog, and geoprocessing.

- Connect to and read numerous common GIS formats—for example, TAB, MIF, E00, and GML—as well as numerous database connections.

- Define complex, semantic data translators using FME Workbench.

- Manipulate and join rich attribute data from many table formats and DBMSs with features.

- Export any feature class to more than 50 output formats—for example, export to GML—and create advanced translators for custom output formats.

A complementary data delivery extension is also available for ArcIMS that enables GIS and data publishers to provide data delivery services for the same range of GIS data formats.

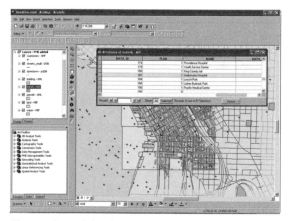

An example of using the ArcGIS Data Interoperability extension in ArcCatalog to convert FME data

Users can drag and drop data sources into ArcMap and make use of all the mapping functions available to native ESRI formats, such as viewing features and attributes, identifying features, and making selections.

The ArcGIS Data Interoperability extension provides direct read access to more than 65 spatial data formats, including GML, DWG/DXF, MicroStation® Design, MapInfo MID/MIF, and TAB.

ArcGIS Geostatistical Analyst

ArcGIS Geostatistical Analyst provides statistical tools for analyzing and mapping continuous data and for surface generation. Exploratory spatial data analysis tools provide different insights about the data: its distribution, global and local outliers, global trends, level of spatial autocorrelation, and variation among multiple datasets.

The ArcGIS Geostatistical Analyst extension's predictions can also measure uncertainty associated with predictions, allowing users to answer questions such as, What is the probability that the ozone levels exceed the Environmental Protection Agency (EPA) standard at the specified location?

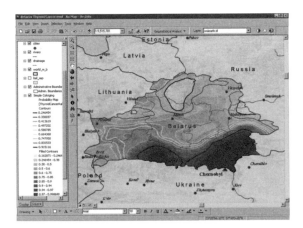

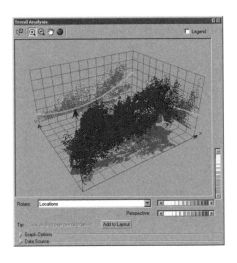

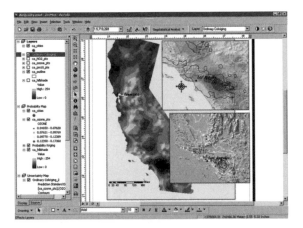

With ArcGIS Geostatistical Analyst, users can quickly and easily generate summary statistics, analyze trends, and graphically represent statistical data for surface estimation.

ArcGIS Network Analyst

ArcGIS Network Analyst is an extension used for routing and network-based spatial analysis (for example, location analysis, drive-time analysis, and spatial interaction modeling). ArcGIS Network Analyst allows ArcGIS Desktop users to model realistic network conditions and scenarios.

ArcGIS Network Analyst supports:

- Drive-time analysis
- Point-to-point routing
- Route directions
- Service area definition
- Shortest path
- Optimum route
- Closest facility
- Origin–Destination

ArcGIS Network Analyst enables ArcGIS users to solve a variety of problems using geographic networks. Many network-based tasks can be performed, such as finding the most efficient travel route or closest facility, generating travel directions, and defining service areas based on travel time.

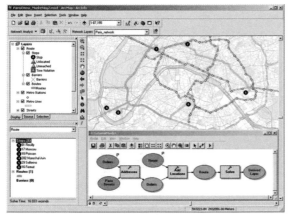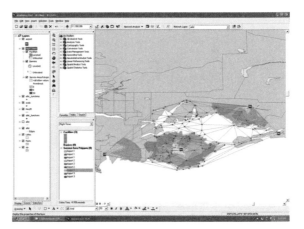

Route and travel time calculations performed with ArcGIS Network Analyst.

ArcGIS Publisher and ArcReader

ArcGIS Publisher is an extension used to publish data, maps, and globes authored using ArcGIS Desktop. ArcGIS Publisher enables the creation of a published map file (PMF) format for any ArcMap document as well as for any Globe document authored using the ArcGIS 3D Analyst extension.

PMFs are used in the free ArcReader application and allow users to share their ArcMap documents with other users. The PMF format can also be used to deploy maps over the Web through ArcIMS and ArcGIS Server.

Adding ArcGIS Publisher to ArcGIS Desktop allows users to open up access to their spatial information to many other users. With ArcMap and ArcGlobe, users can author interactive maps and globes, publish them with ArcGIS Publisher, and share them via ArcReader, ArcGIS Server, and ArcIMS ArcMap Server.

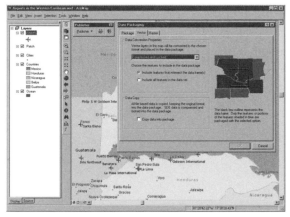

Build PMFs in ArcMap with the ArcGIS Publisher extension.

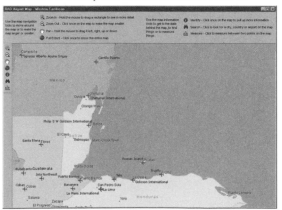

Deliver PMFs freely to any number of users.

What is ArcReader?

ArcReader is a map and globe viewer that can be freely distributed to any number of users. The ArcReader application is included with the ArcGIS Desktop installation media for a number of platforms including Microsoft Windows, Sun™ Solaris™, and Linux® running on Intel® hardware.

ArcGIS Publisher includes a programmable ArcReader control for VB, Visual C++, and .NET developers. This enables users to embed ArcReader in existing applications or build a custom ArcReader for viewing PMFs.

Compressed data that's locked to a PMF can be published with a user name and password as part of an ArcReader project file so that maps and data can be safely shared with authorized users.

ArcReader helps users deploy their GIS in many ways. It opens up access to GIS data; presents information in high-quality, professional looking maps; and provides ArcReader users with the ability to interactively use and print maps, explore and analyze data, and view geographic information with interactive, 3D scenes.

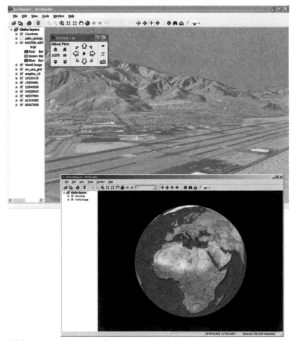

Globe viewing in ArcReader

ArcGIS Schematics

ArcGIS Schematics generates database-driven schematic and geoschematic graphic representations. Whether electrical, gas, telecommunications, or tabular networks, ArcGIS Schematics generates on-demand network graphs and schematics.

A schematic is a view of a GIS network. This extension enables users to draw many graphical views of a network structure and place schematic views in documents and maps.

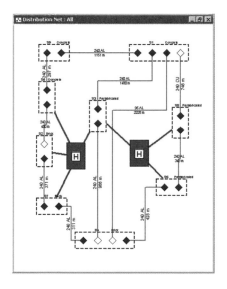

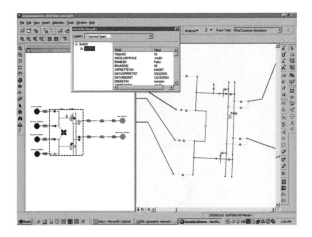

Some examples of ArcGIS Schematics for electric and water networks and homeland security

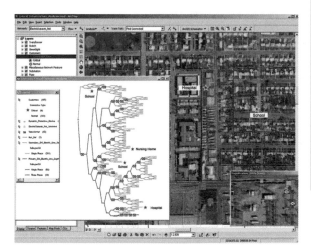

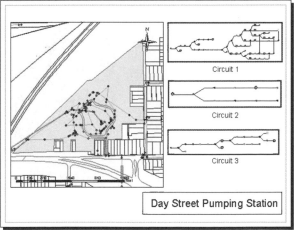

ArcGIS Spatial Analyst

ArcGIS Spatial Analyst provides a broad range of powerful raster modeling and analysis features that allow users to create, query, map, and analyze cell-based raster data. ArcGIS Spatial Analyst also allows integrated raster–vector analysis. With ArcGIS Spatial Analyst, users can derive information about their data, identify spatial relationships, find suitable locations, and calculate the accumulated cost of traveling from one point to another.

ArcGIS Spatial Analyst provides a key toolbox when used with the geoprocessing framework in ArcGIS Desktop.

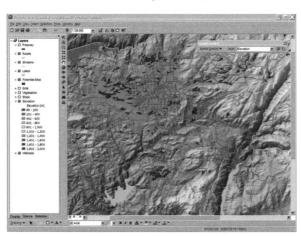

Site suitability analysis

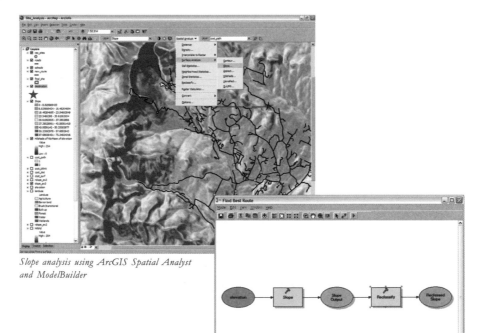

Slope analysis using ArcGIS Spatial Analyst and ModelBuilder

ArcGIS Survey Analyst

For years, numerous survey professionals and GIS practitioners have required the functionality to integrate comprehensive survey information into their GIS and to use surveying as a base to improve as well as quantify the spatial accuracy of their GIS databases. This is the goal of ArcGIS Survey Analyst.

With ArcGIS Survey Analyst, users can manage a comprehensive survey database as an integrated part of

their GIS, including adding updates and improvements from new field surveys over time. The relative accuracy and error in the survey system can be displayed for any survey location. In addition, users can associate feature locations with survey points in the survey system and adjust feature geometry to snap to the survey locations.

ArcGIS Survey Analyst is used by GIS organizations to incrementally improve the spatial accuracy of their GIS data using survey techniques and GPS information.

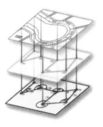

Geographic feature geometry can be linked to survey locations to improve spatial accuracy.

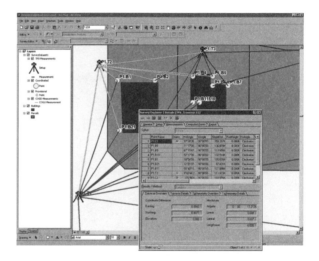

The graphic above shows measurement information and the traverse of the survey network.

ArcGIS Tracking Analyst

ArcGIS Tracking Analyst allows users to view and analyze temporal data; this includes tracking feature movement through time and tracking system values for locations over time.

ArcGIS Tracking Analyst includes:

- Display point and track data (real time and fixed time)

- The ability to symbolize time by color (to show the aging of data)

- Interactive playback

- Actions (based on attribute or spatial queries)

- Highlight capability

- Suppression

- Support for lines and polygons

- Temporal histogram in playback

- The ability to symbolize map layers based on time

- Layer-based time windows to manage many temporal layers

- Temporal offset for comparisons of temporal events

- Animation files

- Data clock for additional analysis

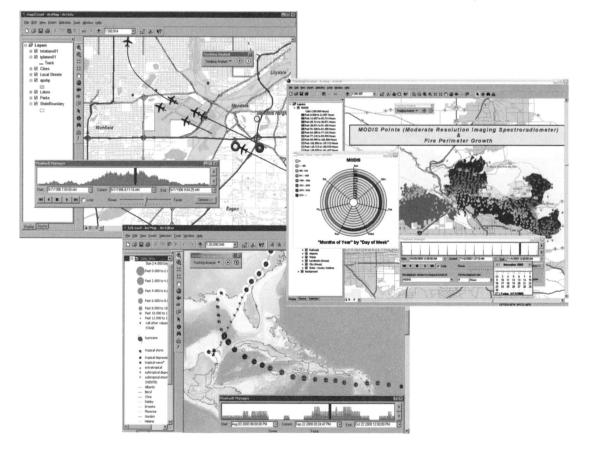

In ArcGIS Tracking Analyst, the interactive Playback Manager (start, stop, pause, rewind) is used to view events through windows.

ArcScan for ArcGIS

ArcScan for ArcGIS adds raster editing and scan digitizing functionality to the editing capabilities in ArcEditor and ArcInfo. It is used to generate data from scanned vector maps and manuscripts. It simplifies the data capture work flow of editing workstations using ArcGIS.

With ArcScan for ArcGIS, users can perform raster-to-vector conversion tasks, including raster editing, raster snapping, manual raster tracing, and batch vectorization.

ArcScan for ArcGIS is included with ArcEditor and ArcInfo, and it is available as an optional extension for ArcView.

Floor plans

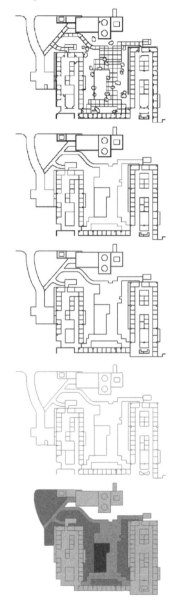

Soil maps

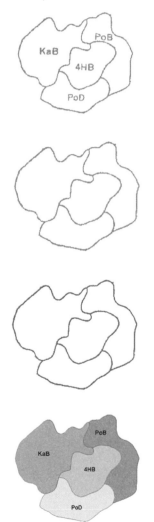

This work flow (top to bottom) shows vectorization examples of floor plans and soil maps. Results were achieved through a combination of raster editing and cleanup followed by scan digitizing.

ArcWeb Services

Web services are increasing in use on the Web for providing both information as well as software logic from dedicated servers. This concept of on-demand computing means that users can plug into existing content and tools and use them in their own applications.

ArcWeb Services provide Web service access to both GIS data content and GIS functions that work in concert with the data services—on demand when needed. This eliminates the overhead of purchasing and maintaining large datasets and provides useful content that developers can embed and consume in Web-based GIS applications and solutions. ArcWeb Services are always available on the Web so that users with strong Internet support can plug in to these services and use them at any time.

General access to ArcWeb Services is sold commercially as a series of credits (in blocks of 100,000 credits). When users access each Web service, they spend a portion of their credits. Each ESRI Developer Network (EDN) subscription includes one block for use in application development, testing, and demonstration.

ArcWeb Services content is provided by a number of key companies including Tele Atlas, Meteorlogix®, GlobeXplorer, Pixxures, National Geographic, ESRI Business Information Systems (ESRI BIS), and TrafficCast.

For more information about EDN, see Chapter 6, 'ESRI Developer Network'.

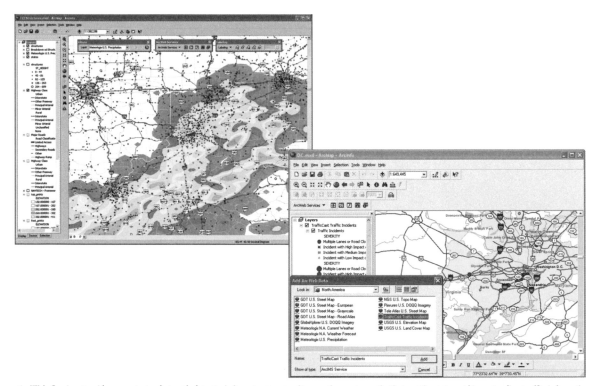

ArcWeb Services provide access to terabytes of data including street maps, live weather maps, orthophotography, topographic maps, live traffic information, shaded relief imagery, flood data, and census data.

Maplex for ArcGIS

Maplex for ArcGIS adds advanced label placement and conflict detection to ArcMap. Maplex for ArcGIS can be used to generate text that is saved with map documents as well as annotation that can be incorporated into comprehensive annotation layers in the geodatabase.

Using Maplex for ArcGIS can save significant production time. Case studies have shown that Maplex for ArcGIS can shave at least 50 percent, and often more, off the time spent on map labeling tasks. Because Maplex for ArcGIS provides better text rendering and print-quality text placement, it is an essential tool for GIS-based cartography. Any GIS site that makes maps should consider having at least one copy of Maplex for ArcGIS.

Maplex for ArcGIS is included with ArcInfo, and it is available as an optional extension for ArcView and ArcEditor.

Labels placed using the ESRI Standard Label Engine

Labels placed with the Maplex for ArcGIS extension

4

Server GIS: ArcSDE, ArcIMS, and ArcGIS Server

Server GIS is rapidly growing for many kinds of centrally hosted GIS computing. Centrally hosted servers in an enterprise or on the Web make it possible for users to work together and share GIS resources.

A shared GIS of a few or an unlimited number of users may have requirements that must be supported:

- Shared data management in DBMSs and files

- A shared catalog that enables other users to search and find published geographic information

- Mapping services to share interactive maps across the Web

- Data delivery services to share data across the Web and for data downloads

- Data editing services

- Geoprocessing services

- Web-based GIS applications

Some GIS users are focused on workgroup and enterprise systems, while others need more than a centralized system for information sharing and collaboration. Many users have begun using GIS Web services for data sharing and Web publishing. Some user communities have established formal frameworks and participate in NSDIs and GSDIs.

These loose federations share GIS content and processing logic through GIS portals on the Web.

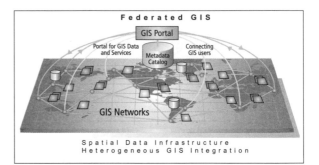

The need for greater collaboration has led to the growth of federated GIS. Federated GIS is based on a distributed collection of heterogeneous GIS nodes that share and use each other's geographic information and services. Catalog portals provide access through a registry of geographic information services and datasets. GIS users register their information services with the portal where other users can search for and find information. Each catalog entry contains a URL or access location for the registered information sets and services, enabling information from multiple users to be combined across the Web through the use of standards-based Web services.

WHAT IS A GIS SERVER?

GIS software can be centralized in application servers and Web servers to deliver GIS capabilities to any number of users over networks and across the Web. This typically begins with data sharing and server-based Web mapping applications but is growing to include a broad range of GIS functionality. Comprehensive GIS capabilities must be provided to support these broad GIS server requirements. For example, GIS servers can be used for:

- Managing large GIS databases

- Internet delivery of geographic information

- Hosting central GIS catalog portals for information discovery and use

- Building and deploying browser-based Web applications that can be hosted centrally but accessed through any Web browser

- Centrally hosting critical GIS functions that are accessed by many users in an organization

- Back-office processing of enterprise GIS databases

- Distributed GIS computing, such as distributed GIS data management and analysis

- Internet delivery of comprehensive GIS functionality

- Interoperability of heterogeneous GIS nodes through the use of standard Web services protocols based on XML

ESRI's GIS servers comply with numerous IT, Web, and GIS industry standards. They operate with other enterprise software, such as Web servers; DBMSs; enterprise application frameworks, such as J2EE and Microsoft .NET; and in services-oriented architectures. This enables the integration of GIS with numerous information system technologies and computing standards.

ArcGIS offers three server products: ArcSDE, ArcIMS, and ArcGIS Server.

ArcSDE

ArcSDE is an advanced spatial data server, providing a gateway for using, managing, and storing spatial data in a DBMS for any client application—for example, ArcIMS or ArcGIS Desktop.

ArcIMS

ArcIMS is a scalable Internet map server. It is widely used for GIS Web publishing to deliver maps, data, and metadata to Web users. For example, ArcIMS provides browser-based access to many GIS catalog portals that enable users to publish and share geographic knowledge with other users.

ArcGIS Server

ArcGIS Server is a comprehensive GIS toolkit for enterprise and Web application developers. It is used to build distributed and multitier enterprise information system configurations.

GIS Server Functionality		ArcSDE	ArcIMS	ArcGIS Server
Multiuser data management in a DBMS		X		
Multitier, configurable GIS data server		X		
Support for multiple DBMSs		X		
Support for long transactions and versions		X		
GIS Web publishing	-Maps		X	
	-Data		X	
	-Metadata (XML-based services)		X	
HTML mapping application			X	X
Java mapping application			X	X
ASP and JSP support for developers			X	X
Metadata catalog management and search			X	
Support for Web interoperability			X	X
Support for OGC interoperability		X	X	X
Support for data interoperability			X	X
Web application development framework for .NET, ASP, and Java JSP				X
Data access and update API				X
Server-based GIS editing				X
Distributed data management	-Download/Upload			X
	-Extract/Insert			X
	-Replication			X
GIS analysis in a central server				X
Comprehensive ArcObjects library for enterprise and Web developers				X
SOAP-based GIS Web services				X
Optional raster analysis				X
Optional network analysis				X
Optional terrain/3D analysis				X

Server GIS functionality in the three ArcGIS server products

ArcSDE is the GIS gateway to relational databases for ArcGIS. It allows users to manage geographic information in any of several DBMSs and serve their data openly to all ArcGIS applications.

ArcSDE is a key component in a multiuser ArcGIS system. It provides an open interface to the DBMS and allows ArcGIS to manage geographic information on several database platforms including Oracle, Microsoft SQL Server, IBM DB2, and Informix.

When users need a large multiuser geodatabase that can be edited and used simultaneously by many users, ArcSDE adds the necessary capabilities to their ArcGIS system by enabling them to manage a shared, multiuser geodatabase in a DBMS. It does this by adding a host of fundamental GIS capabilities, detailed in the table below.

ArcSDE capabilities

High performance DBMS gateway	ArcSDE is a gateway to many DBMSs. It is not a relational database or a storage model. Instead, it is an interface that supports advanced, high performance GIS data management on a number of DBMS platforms.
Open DBMS support	ArcSDE allows you to manage geographic information in a number of DBMSs: Oracle, Oracle with Locator, Microsoft SQL Server, Informix, and IBM DB2.
Multiuser	ArcSDE enables large geodatabase support for many users and supports multiuser editing.
Continuous, scalable databases	ArcSDE can support massive geodatabases and any number of users up to the DBMS limits.
GIS work flows and long transactions	Data management work flows in GIS, such as multiuser editing, history, check-out/check-in, and loosely coupled replication, rely on long transactions and versioning. ArcSDE provides this support across the DBMS.
Comprehensive geographic information modeling	ArcSDE ensures high integrity data storage of feature and raster geometries in the DBMS, including well-formed feature and raster geometries, support for x,y,z and x,y,z,m coordinates, curves, solids, multirow rasters, topologies, networks, annotation, metadata, geoprocessing models, maps, layers, and so on.
Flexible configuration	The ArcSDE gateway logic supports several multitier configuration options for application servers within client applications and across networks and computers. ArcSDE is supported for a broad range of Windows, UNIX, and Linux operating systems.

ArcSDE plays an important role in a multiuser GIS by providing a number of fundamental capabilities.

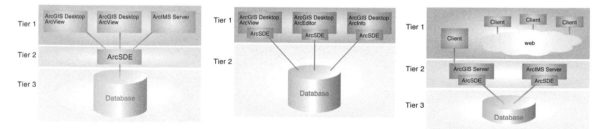

ArcSDE acts as the gateway between ArcGIS and a relational database, and it can be configured in many ways.

WHY USE ArcSDE?

ArcSDE enables the same capabilities on all DBMSs. Although all relational database vendors support Structured Query Language (SQL) and will process simple SQL in similar ways, there are significant differences among database vendors in the details of their database server implementation. These relate to performance and indexing, the supported data types, the integrity management tools, and the execution of complex queries. These also relate to support for spatial types in the DBMS.

Standard SQL does not support spatial data. The ISO SQL/MM Spatial and OGC's simple feature SQL specifications extend SQL by defining standard SQL language for vector geometry types. DB2 and Informix support these standard SQL types. Oracle has implemented its own independent spatial type system as an option that costs extra, and Microsoft SQL Server has no spatial type support. ArcSDE provides the flexibility to leverage the unique capabilities that each DBMS vendor offers, yet it provides the necessary support in the underlying DBMS when it does not exist.

ArcSDE supports very high performance management of spatial data on the leading database configurations:

- Oracle (with compressed binary)

- Oracle (with Locator or Spatial)

- Microsoft SQL Server (with compressed binary)

- IBM DB2 (with the Spatial Extender)

- IBM Informix (with Spatial DataBlade®)

ArcSDE exists to deal with the diversity and complexity in the underlying DBMS world. The ArcSDE architecture provides great flexibility for users. It allows an open choice of database vendors and physical schemas as well as highly tuned data access and spatial integrity on each relational database engine.

ArcSDE SHARES RESPONSIBILITIES BETWEEN THE DBMS AND GIS

Responsibility for management of geographic datasets is shared between GIS software and generic DBMS software. Certain aspects of geographic dataset management, such as disk-based storage, definition of attribute types, associative query processing, and multiuser transaction processing, are delegated to the DBMS. Some DBMS engines have been extended with support for spatial types, associated indexing, search functionality, and SQL support for simple spatial queries.

The GIS application retains responsibility for defining the specific DBMS schema used to represent various geographic datasets and for domain-specific logic, which maintains the integrity and utility of the underlying records. In effect, the DBMS is used as an implementation mechanism for geographic datasets.

ArcSDE is based on a multitier architecture (application and storage), where aspects related to data storage and retrieval are implemented in the storage (DBMS) tier, and high-level data integrity and information processing functions are retained in the application and domain software (ArcGIS).

ArcSDE supports the ArcGIS application tier and provides DBMS gateway technology, enabling support for geodatabase storage in numerous DBMSs. ArcSDE is used for efficiently storing, indexing, and accessing vector, raster, survey, metadata, and other spatial data maintained in the DBMS.

ArcSDE also ensures that full GIS functionality is available regardless of the capabilities in the underlying DBMS and applies this logic consistently across all DBMSs. Users can expect that core underlying DBMS technology will be sufficient for managing their geodata resources.

ArcSDE manages the underlying geometry storage in DBMS tables using each DBMS's supported data types, which are accessible through SQL in the DBMS.

ArcSDE also provides an openly published ArcSDE client library enabling complete access to the underlying spatial tables for custom applications. The application programming interface (API) is available for both C and Java.

This flexibility means an open, scalable solution; more choices for users; and better interoperability.

ArcSDE Advantages
· High performance
· Extremely large data volumes
· Integrated long transactions and versions
· Supports all GIS data (vector, raster, survey, terrains, metadata, and others)
· Supports leading RDBMSs consistently
· Scales to many users and databases

Fit GIS into a coherent IT strategy

Many GIS users require that their GIS fits into a coherent information technology strategy for their organization. Simply put, their GIS must adhere to IT standards, the GIS data should be managed as an integral part of the organization's data holdings, the data must be secure, and access to this data must be controlled, yet it should be open and easy as well. These are standard advantages of a DBMS that GIS users need. The main role of ArcSDE and the geodatabase is to manage the integration between the GIS and DBMS.

Grow your GIS

Geodatabases can scale from small, single-user databases to large, enterprisewide, multiuser databases. The primary role of ArcSDE is to enable the geodatabase to be shared by many users across any network, enable any number of users to edit and use the GIS datasets, and scale the geodatabase size to any level necessary to meet user requirements.

SPATIAL GEOMETRY STORAGE

ArcSDE does nothing exotic in the DBMS for data management. It takes full advantage of generic DBMS capabilities and SQL data types.

ArcSDE enables access to many DBMSs, manages data in the set of standard SQL types supported in each DBMS, and supports all spatial data—including features; rasters; topologies; networks; terrains; surveys; tabular information; and location data, such as addresses, models, and metadata—regardless of the underlying DBMS.

ArcSDE uses the supplied SQL types for data storage and fully supports extended spatial types for SQL when the underlying DBMS supports them. Binary large object types are used if the DBMS does not support extended spatial types.

DBMS	Geometry Storage	RDBMS Column Type	Notes
SQL Server	ArcSDE Compressed Binary	Image	Microsoft SQL Server does not support extended data types for spatial. However, its binary type, called an Image column, fully manages the complex binary data streams, as required for complex line and polygon features found in typical and advanced GIS applications. SQL Server binary types have proven to be as robust, scalable, and high performing as the other enterprise RDBMSs.
	OGC Well-Known Binary	Image	OGC Simple Features Type.
IBM DB2	Spatial Extender—Geometry Object	ST_Geometry [1]	Both IBM RDBMS offerings, DB2 and Informix, utilize extended spatial types for managing vector geometry. These were built in concert with ESRI and are based on the ISO SQL MM specification for spatial.
Informix	Spatial Database—Geometry Object	ST_Geometry	
Oracle	Numerous Options: 1. ArcSDE Compressed Binary	Long Raw	This ArcSDE storage mechanism is used by default, and it is the most commonly used data storage mechanism. It provides high performance, scalability, and reliability.
	2. LOB	LOB	Some users deploy LOBs to use Oracle Replication Services.
	3. OGC Well-Known Binary	LOB	OGC Simple Features Type.
Oracle with Spatial Option or the Locator Option	Oracle Spatial Geometry Type	SDO_Geometry [1]	In addition to using the ArcSDE compressed binary or LOB types, Oracle Locator and Oracle Spatial customers can optionally use the SDO_Geometry column type. Users can make this decision on a table-by-table basis, enabling them to use the best option for each individual dataset.

1. ST_Geometry and SDO_Geometry actually refer to a collection of types for points, lines, and polygons.

Access to multiple GIS datasets

GIS data management and compilation requires more than a single, large enterprise database. A major requirement in any GIS is the ability to simultaneously access many databases and files in many formats, DBMSs, and networks. ArcSDE helps meet this key GIS requirement by not tying users to a single DBMS or data management solution.

Fundamental technology for multiuser geodatabases

ArcSDE is the gateway that enables the geodatabase application logic to operate on geodatabases that can be persisted in relational databases. The geodatabase software provides advanced behavior and integrity, while ArcSDE enables efficient storage and access in numerous alternate DBMS architectures.

ArcSDE ADVANTAGES

Case studies and performance tests have demonstrated that ArcSDE performs and scales better than any other DBMS solution. In addition, ArcSDE is the most open, interoperable framework for managing geographic information within a DBMS, because it supports and scales across a range of DBMS platforms, implements both ISO and OGC simple features, supports the ISO SQL standards for spatial, has openly published Import and Export formats, and has developer APIs available for use by any site. ArcSDE is integrated with most leading GIS applications.

An information system includes more than a data store and persistence mechanism. It also requires the comprehensive, integrated GIS logic and functionality that is provided by ArcGIS.

ArcSDE has proven itself by all technical measures in benchmark situations. When users require a high-performance, scalable, multiuser GIS database solution, ArcSDE is the solution of choice.

GIS WEB PUBLISHING OF MAPS, DATA, AND METADATA

ArcIMS provides Web publishing of GIS maps, data, and metadata in a central Web portal for access by many users, both inside the organization as well as outside, on the Web.

ArcIMS enables Web sites to serve GIS data, interactive maps, metadata catalogs, and focused GIS applications.

Typically, ArcIMS users access these GIS services through their Web browsers using HTML or Java applications that are included with ArcIMS. In addition, ArcIMS services can be accessed using a wide range of clients including ArcGIS Desktop, ArcGIS Engine seats, ArcReader applications, ArcPad applications, ArcGIS Server nodes, MapObjects® for Java applications, and many wireless devices that use HTTP and XML for Web communications.

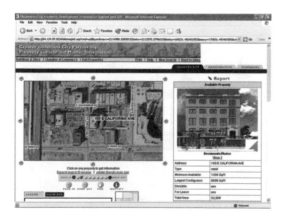

ArcIMS is used for GIS Web publishing to deliver maps, data, and metadata on the Web. Users most commonly access ArcIMS services using their Web browsers and ArcGIS software seats.

HOW IS ArcIMS USED?

ArcIMS is used for GIS Web publishing. Its primary focus is Web delivery of geographic data, maps, and metadata. The following three examples illustrate the main application functions of ArcIMS.

Focused application delivery

Most ArcIMS users need to deliver GIS to numerous internal users or to external users on the Internet. The requirement is to provide data access and simple, focused data use applications to users through a Web browser. Users perform the same basic tasks in these Web applications. For example, ArcIMS is excellent at publishing status maps for the public showing the state of particular events and outbreaks, such as SARS and West Nile virus, as well as providing a host of e-government applications for citizens. E-gov applications include parcel tax review, permitting, and mapping of high-interest public information such as crime, city development plans, school districts, voter polling places, and so on.

Such applications share some common characteristics. There are many users, and the application must be able to scale from minor to very heavy use with perhaps millions of Web hits per day. The interfaces to these applications are focused. The application users tend to do a small number of very focused tasks. The applications combine and publish GIS information to many users. With ArcIMS, they aren't typically used for data update or advanced, ad hoc GIS analysis.

A National Weather Service Web site for hurricanes

A British Geological Survey Web site

Publishing for professional GIS users

Many organizations publish a series of GIS data feeds for GIS professionals within, as well as outside, their organization. Such ArcIMS applications are focused on data sharing between GIS professionals. The intended uses of the data are not necessarily well known ahead of time and can vary from user to user. GIS professionals fuse this data to their GIS, along with other information sets, to accomplish many tasks.

ArcGIS Desktop accesses data using ArcIMS servers to enrich maps and integrate remote information into work.

Technology for GIS networks

GIS Web publishing with ArcIMS is often the initial step in the implementation of enterprise GIS. GIS organizations initially publish and deliver GIS data and services to a broad audience, often outside their own department. The ArcIMS technology can then be complemented by adding ArcGIS Server technology for centrally focused data compilation and management as well as advanced, server-based GIS modeling and analysis.

Many GIS users recognize that GIS data moves through networks. A GIS network is a loosely coupled federation of GIS nodes where GIS data and Web services are published by numerous organizations. An exciting trend and vision in GIS is the development of national, continental, and global SDIs where many users register their GIS datasets, information, and activities at a common catalog portal. A GIS catalog portal can be searched, much like an Internet search might be performed at www.google.com, to discover and gain access to GIS information relevant for a specific use.

ArcIMS is a key GIS technology for building all the parts of a GIS network. ArcIMS includes tools for building a GIS portal with a metadata catalog, catalog search and discovery services for the Web, data and metadata harvesting services, gazetteer services, and Web mapping applications.

The optional GIS Portal Toolkit extension is available for building and managing GIS catalog portals. Numerous organizations have begun to publish SDI nodes for their organizations using the GIS Portal Toolkit extension.

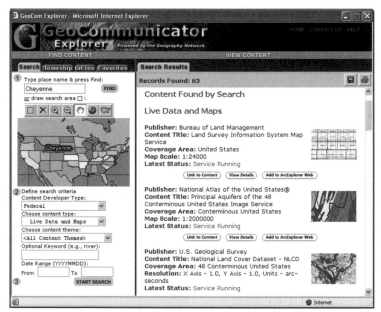

The United States Bureau of Land Management (BLM) and the U.S. Forest Service (USFS) host a site named GeoCommunicator that serves land records and land management datasets.

ArcIMS CAPABILITIES

When an ArcIMS client sends a request to a server, the ArcIMS server processes and responds to the request. Typical ArcIMS requests generate maps, retrieve geographic data for a given map extent, or perform a metadata search. A range of GIS Web delivery services are available through ArcIMS. The most common ArcIMS services deliver interactive maps to many types of clients.

When a user creates a map for their Web site, they determine which data layers to include and how map features will be rendered. They define symbology, add labels, set scale factors, and so on. When a client sends a request for a map, it is generated on the server based on their specifications. The map is delivered to the client in any of three services: as an image, streamed features, or an ArcMap Image Service.

An image service uses the ArcIMS image rendering capabilities to deliver a snapshot of the map to the requesting client. The snapshot is sent as a compressed image file. A new map image is generated each time the client requests new information—for example, to pan the map. The image service can also deliver compressed raster data to clients. Image services can use either of two protocols: ArcXML or the OGC WMS specification.

A feature service streams compressed vector features to the requesting client. Feature streaming enables more advanced client-side tasks, such as feature labeling, feature symbolization, MapTip creation, and spatial selection of features. This functionality allows the user on the client side to change the appearance of the map. Feature services can use either of two protocols: ArcXML or the OGC WFS specification.

An ArcMap Image Service streams images from an ArcMap document to the requesting client. This service enables users to deliver maps that use the advanced cartographic and open data access capabilities of ArcMap. Virtually any information and graphic representations that is created in ArcMap can be served using the ArcMap Server. The ArcMap Server also supports access to versioned geodatabases and is used in many enterprise GIS scenarios. An ArcMap Image Service can use either of two protocols: ArcXML or the OGC WMS specification.

Here is a list of some of the key GIS Web publishing capabilities of ArcIMS:

Image rendering

Image rendering creates a snapshot of the current view of an interactive map. For example, as a user interactively pans and zooms on a map or turns map layers on and off, an ArcIMS map server renders each view and delivers it as an image to ArcIMS clients.

Feature streaming

Feature streaming involves streaming vector features to clients, enabling a number of client-side tasks: feature labeling, MapTip creation, spatial selection, and so on. Feature streaming is important for more advanced ArcIMS clients including ArcExplorer™—Java Edition, ArcGIS Desktop, and the ArcIMS Java viewers. Streamed features from ArcIMS Web sites can be integrated with other features, such as local data, and used together in analysis.

Data query

Users can build new queries or run predefined queries to derive specific information. The client submits the query to the server, and the server returns the query results to the client.

Data extraction

Users can request geographic datasets from the server. The server responds to a request for data by sending zipped data files in a selected format to the client (for example, as shapefiles) for local use.

Geocoding

This allows users to submit an address and receive a location from the ArcIMS geocoding service. Based on the address input, the server either returns the location of an exact match to the address or a list of candidate matches.

Metadata catalog services

A catalog that references data holdings and information sets can be created using ArcGIS Desktop, ArcIMS, and ArcSDE and published as a search service using ArcIMS. This allows users to provide an open search mechanism for other users to find and access GIS information at their Web site. They can create a clearinghouse, and they can participate in a GIS network with other users.

Metadata catalog browse and search applications

A series of Web-based HTML applications is included with ArcIMS for performing metadata catalog searches. This also includes a customizable gazetteer. These application tools are important for building a GIS catalog portal.

ArcMap Server

ArcGIS can be used to author maps, then serve them using ArcIMS. This enables access to advanced geodatabases and ArcMap cartography in an ArcIMS Web site.

Web mapping applications

ArcIMS includes a series of Web mapping applications for browser-based GIS access. Use of Web browsers as GIS terminals opens up access to many new users.

OGC interoperability support

ArcIMS provides broad ongoing support for many OGC specifications, such as WMS, WFS, WCS, and CS-W.

OPTIONAL EXTENSIONS FOR ArcIMS

The Web publishing capabilities in a GIS Web site can be enhanced through a series of optional ArcIMS product extensions.

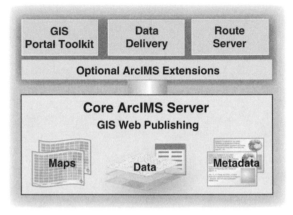

Optional extensions that add capabilities to ArcIMS Web sites

GIS Portal Toolkit

The GIS Portal Toolkit extension is a technology and services solution for implementing local, regional, national, and global SDI portals. GIS portals organize content and services such as directories, search tools, community information, support resources, data, and applications. They provide capabilities to query metadata records for relevant data and services and link directly to the online sites that host content services. The content can be viewed as maps and used in geographic queries and analyses.

GIS Portal Toolkit provides all the tools and templates to create a GIS portal. Based on ESRI's ArcIMS and ArcSDE software, this standards-based solution offered through ESRI Professional Services is a cost-effective way to get a functional site up and running quickly.

The key elements of GIS Portal Toolkit are:

*   Portal Web Site Template—A collection of template Web pages, scripts, and content that constitutes a functional draft of a GIS portal Web site. The template provides tools to perform a number of tasks, such as building a user interface to the site, hosting user-supplied content in the form of Web pages, and querying content.

- Map Viewer—A browser-based map data viewer that can combine data services from one or more portal servers. Map Viewer has extensive functionality for map navigation, printing, selection queries, data exploration, direct use of online Web services, and fusing multiple services into a single map.

- Metadata Catalog—A searchable repository that can store, update, and retrieve metadata.

Data Delivery Extension

ArcIMS Data Delivery Extension enables ArcIMS sites to deliver data downloads in any number of GIS data formats, including complex data translators defined with the ArcGIS Data Interoperability extension. ArcIMS Data Delivery Extension is based on Safe Software's FME suite for advanced spatial data translation.

Route Server

The ArcIMS Route Server extension provides a countrywide navigation street database to support optimal routing and geocoding services on the street data.

DEVELOPING ArcIMS APPLICATIONS WITH ArcXML

ArcIMS uses XML for its communications and interactions. The openly published XML language for ArcIMS is named ArcXML. It provides access to all ArcIMS functions and capabilities. All client requests and server responses in ArcIMS are coded in ArcXML.

Many ArcIMS developers program Web applications using ArcXML to customize and extend core ArcIMS capabilities.

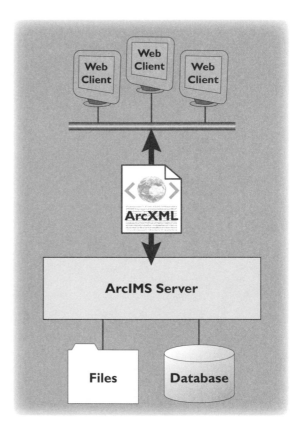

ArcXML also supports a series of connectors that enable Web developers to use standard tools, including ColdFusion®, Active Server Pages (ASP) for Microsoft developers, and JavaServer Pages (JSP) to build Web applications using J2EE.

ArcIMS SUPPORT FOR GIS INTEROPERABILITY

ArcIMS plays a key role by supporting many Web services protocols for IT and GIS. It is important that GIS users can offer interoperability choices to their users via various specifications including XML, SOAP, WMS, WFS, GML, WCS, catalog services, Z39.50, and so on. ArcIMS supports most GIS and IT Web services standards.

ArcGIS Server is a platform for building enterprise GIS applications that are centrally managed, support multiple users, include advanced GIS functionality, and are built using industry standards. ArcGIS Server manages comprehensive GIS functionality, such as maps, locators, and software objects for use in central server applications.

With ArcGIS Server users can:

- Provide browser-based access to GIS

- Deliver advanced GIS Web services throughout an organization

- Develop custom applications using .NET or Java to meet specific needs

- Integrate GIS and other IT technologies using industry-standard software

- Provide centrally managed, multiuser editing capabilities

- Perform focused spatial analysis operations on a server

Developers can use ArcGIS Server to build Web applications, Web services, and other enterprise applications, such as Enterprise JavaBeans (EJBs), that run within standard .NET and J2EE Web servers. ArcGIS Server is also accessed by desktop applications that interact with the server in a client/server mode. ArcGIS Server administration is performed using ArcGIS Desktop, which can be used to access ArcGIS Server over a local area network (LAN) or the Internet.

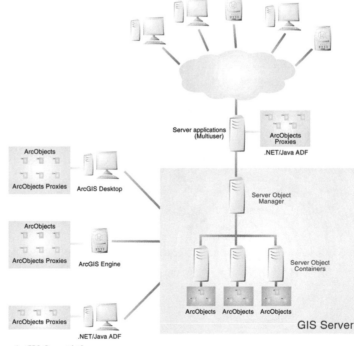

ArcGIS Server platform

ArcGIS Server consists of two primary components: a GIS server and the Web Application Development Framework (ADF™) for .NET and Java. The GIS server hosts ArcObjects for use by Web and enterprise applications. It includes the core ArcObjects library and provides a scalable environment for running ArcObjects in a central, shared server. ADF allows users to build and deploy .NET or Java desktop and Web applications that use ArcObjects running within the GIS server.

.NET ASP and Java JSP applications for GIS can be quickly assembled using ADF because ADF contains a number of user interface tools and Web controls along with access to all the ArcObjects software components.

These can be used to build powerful GIS applications that are hosted and run on a Web server and can be accessed by users through their Web browsers without downloading any special software.

ADF includes a software developer kit with software objects, Web controls, Web application templates, developer help, and code samples. It also includes a Web application runtime for deploying Web applications without having to install ArcObjects on the Web server.

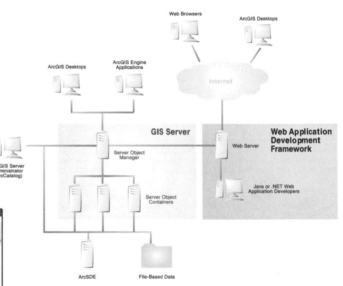

ArcGIS Server provides ArcObjects functionality for both Web applications and client/server application development.

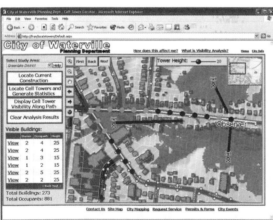

A map created in ArcMap can be easily embedded in a Web mapping application using ADF and a GIS server. Many users can access this mapping application, which is run on a central Web server via their Web browser.

STANDARD GIS SERVER FRAMEWORK

ArcGIS Server provides an industry-standard framework for developing GIS server applications. ArcGIS Desktop (ArcView, ArcEditor, and ArcInfo) and ArcGIS Engine are built from the same set of software objects.

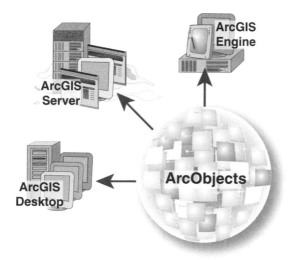

ENTERPRISE GIS DEVELOPMENT TOOLS

ArcGIS Server developers have access to a rich set of GIS software components, including a collection of visual Web controls with events and methods for cross platform customization supporting a variety of development languages.

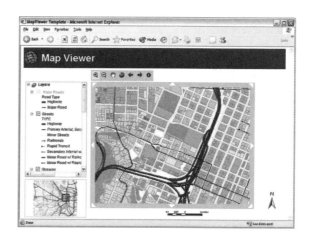

CENTRALLY MANAGED GIS

ArcGIS Server allows the creation of a centrally managed enterprise GIS, delivering Web applications and services to support many users efficiently.

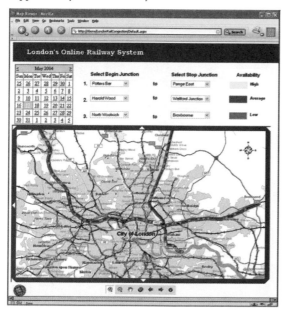

CROSS PLATFORM FUNCTIONALITY

ArcGIS Server ADF supports .NET, Java, and numerous Web servers, allowing users to create applications on a variety of Windows and UNIX platforms.

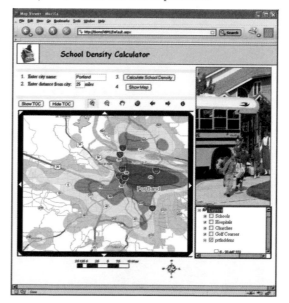

DEVELOPER RESOURCES

ArcGIS Server includes ArcGIS SDK, a collection of diagrams, utilities, add-ins, samples, and documentation to help developers implement custom ArcGIS functionality.

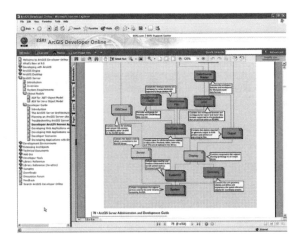

ArcGIS Server is a centrally managed GIS for advanced GIS applications. It enables developers and system designers to implement a central GIS that can be accessed by multiple users. Centralizing GIS applications (such as Web applications) can reduce the costs of installing and administering desktop applications on each user's machine.

The ability of ArcGIS Server to leverage Web services is important for integrating GIS with other IT systems, such as relational databases, Web servers, and enterprise applications servers.

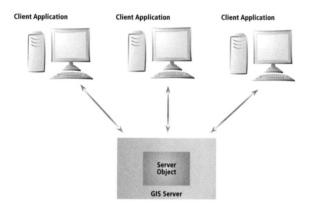

A central GIS server can deliver GIS access to users through their Web browsers and other lightweight clients. ArcGIS Server simplifies multiuser system administration and lowers costs for large multiuser systems.

ArcGIS Server provides browser-based access to GIS; central, multiuser geodatabase editing; distributed data management; focused geoprocessing operations on a server; the ability to publish GIS Web services; and the integration of GIS and IT.

BROWSER-BASED ACCESS TO GIS

Many users will connect via an Internet browser to a Web application written and deployed with ArcGIS Server. These users will interact with the Web application, typically using their Web browsers to access the GIS. Web application users may have little or no knowledge that they are using GIS functionality provided by the GIS server, or they may use their Web browser to access GIS in traditional GIS applications that are centralized in the server.

ArcGIS Server provides the Web ADF for .NET and Java for developers to build browser-based GIS applications. A series of Web controls and application templates are provided for building these custom applications.

CENTRAL, MULTIUSER GEODATABASE EDITING

Enterprise geodatabase management is a major goal for many GIS organizations who need to provide editing and update access to many simultaneous editors. Many of these editors will remotely update the central database through their Web browsers and focused editing applications.

ArcGIS Server provides the framework to ensure that remote editors can make their updates directly to the multiuser geodatabase while maintaining data integrity.

Shown above is an example of browser-based editing of agricultural information built with ArcGIS Server. In this application, agricultural field agents use their Web browsers to add conservation plan features (such as drip irrigation and wind breaks) to a central, multiuser geodatabase.

DISTRIBUTED DATA MANAGEMENT USING VERSIONED ENTERPRISE GEODATABASES

ArcGIS Server provides a central geodatabase application server that can orchestrate distributed data management work flows between a series of GIS systems. The central GIS application server manages geospatial data integrity by providing comprehensive geodatabase logic for all database transactions. For example:

- Some users need the ability to perform disconnected editing. They need to check out portions of the GIS database; edit the data in a separate, standalone GIS system; and post the changes back into the enterprise database.

- Other users need to replicate their geodatabases at a number of locations in independent, standalone systems. Periodically, each instance needs to send and receive the most recent changes to synchronize each replica's contents.

FOCUSED GEOPROCESSING OPERATIONS ON A SERVER

Many users want access to advanced GIS logic to perform analytical and spatial query operations on a central enterprise geodatabase. For example, users need access to functions that can perform advanced GIS logic to:

- Locate events along linear features using linear referencing

- Geocode and locate addresses

- Perform tracing on facilities networks

- Buffer, overlay, and extract features

ArcGIS Server facilitates access to comprehensive GIS logic to support these and many other spatial operations.

PUBLISHING ADVANCED GIS WEB SERVICES

ArcGIS Server includes a SOAP toolkit for building and hosting custom Web services that support request handling using an XML API. Developers can expose GIS functions in ArcObjects as SOAP Web services and can access Web services through distributed computing frameworks on the Internet.

For example, focused Web services can be built to:

- Find the nearest hospital that meets specific conditions (having a certain number of beds, specialists on staff, and so on)

- Locate an address and perform address validation

- Perform queries against central geodatabases

INTEGRATING GIS AND IT

ArcGIS Server is IT-compliant and supports a number of computing technology standards, enabling it to work well with other enterprise information technology. ArcGIS Server supports multitier computing; DBMS access and use; enterprise application servers, such as .NET and J2EE, and a number of developer APIs (C++, COM, .NET, Java, and SOAP) to build and integrate GIS logic with other enterprise technology.

ArcGIS Server contains developer access to complete ArcGIS functionality in a server environment.

Here are some of the key features of ArcGIS Server.

STANDARD GIS FRAMEWORK

ArcGIS Server provides a standard framework for developing GIS server applications. ArcGIS Desktop (ArcView, ArcEditor, and ArcInfo), as well as ArcGIS Engine, are built from this same set of software objects. ArcGIS Server is extensible. Its rich functionality allows developers to concentrate on customizing their GIS implementation instead of focusing on building GIS functionality from scratch.

CENTRALLY MANAGED GIS

ArcGIS Server supports centrally managed enterprise GIS, such as Web applications running on servers, to support many users. For example, Web server applications can run on multiple Web servers to support any number of users.

WEB CONTROLS

ArcGIS Server provides a set of Web controls. These Web controls simplify the programming model for embedding GIS functionality (such as interactive mapping) in your Web application and enable developers to add other advanced GIS functionality to their Web applications.

WEB APPLICATION TEMPLATES

ArcGIS Server includes a set of Web application templates that provide a jump start for developers who want to build Web applications. The Web application templates also provide examples of how to use the Web controls to build Web applications.

CROSS PLATFORM FUNCTIONALITY

ArcGIS Server is supported on Windows, Sun Solaris, and Linux platforms and supports numerous Web servers. The ArcGIS Server ADF supports .NET and Java Web application development on Windows Server platforms and Java on Sun Solaris and Linux servers.

SUPPORT FOR STANDARD DEVELOPER LANGUAGES

ArcGIS Server supports a variety of developer languages including:

- .NET and Java for building Web applications and Web services

- COM and .NET for extending the GIS server with custom components

- COM, .NET, Java, and C++ for building desktop client applications

This enables programming using a wide range of tools. Programming staff can use the languages with which they are familiar.

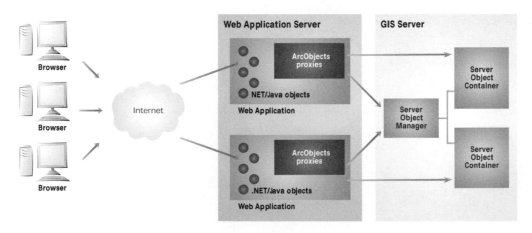

ArcGIS Server architecture

A series of optional extensions are available for ArcGIS Server that add capabilities to the core system. These optional extensions are described briefly below.

SPATIAL

The ArcGIS Server Spatial extension provides a powerful set of functions that allows users to create, query, and analyze cell-based raster data. They can use the Spatial extension to derive information about their data, identify spatial relationships, find suitable locations, calculate travel cost surfaces, and perform a wide range of additional raster geoprocessing operations in ArcGIS Server.

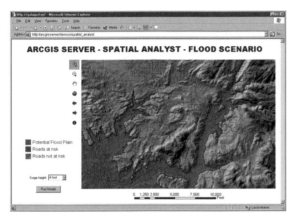

The Spatial extension for ArcGIS Server allows users to create and analyze cell-based raster data. Functions include viewshed, slope, aspect, hillshade analysis, and so on.

3D

The ArcGIS Server 3D extension provides a set of 3D GIS functions to create and analyze surfaces.

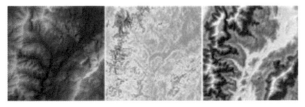

The 3D extension for ArcGIS Server provides a powerful set of tools that allows users to create, query, and analyze surface data.

NETWORK

The ArcGIS Server Network extension provides a complete set of network analysis and mapping functions on the central server.

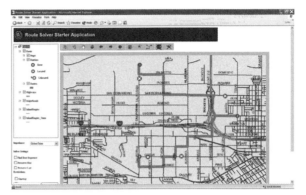

The Network extension for ArcGIS Server provides tools for routing and network-based spatial analysis.

5 Embedded GIS: ArcGIS Engine

In many cases, users require GIS access through intermediate means—for example, helper applications, focused GIS applications, and mobile devices—as well as through high-end professional GIS desktops or simple Web browsers connected to Internet servers.

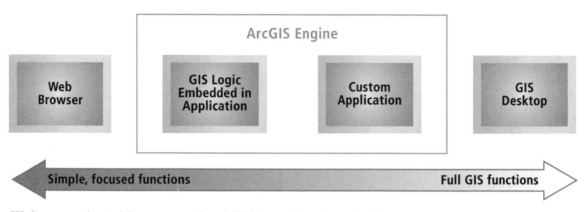

GIS clients can range from simple browser access to professional GIS desktops, such as ArcView and ArcInfo. ArcGIS Engine provides the capability to embed GIS logic in intermediate applications.

Typical examples of intermediate GIS use can range from access to GIS functions within custom applications that are somewhere in between simple Web browsers to high-end GIS desktops. For example:

- As helper applications within Web browsers

- Through GIS functions embedded within word processing documents and spreadsheets

- With focused GIS applications that behave much like ArcView yet support a specific subset of advanced functions (a customized "ArcView Lite" application)

These applications require simple, focused user interfaces. However, they access advanced GIS logic to perform a few specific tasks. For example, many organizations have simple data editors that do not require a full GIS desktop.

Custom GIS applications are also typically highly customized. The user interfaces are built to deliver GIS functions to many users not familiar with GIS. Hence, software developers require a programmable GIS toolkit that enables them to leverage common GIS functions in building their applications.

ArcGIS Engine provides tools to meet these requirements. It provides embeddable GIS components that can be used to build applications to deliver subsets of GIS logic to any number of users within an organization. ArcGIS Engine is infrastructure for delivering any critical subset of GIS capabilities that are relevant to each user's specialized needs.

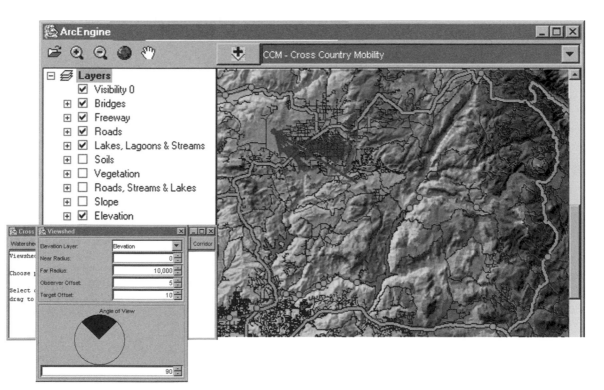

ArcGIS Engine viewshed application

ArcGIS Engine is a comprehensive library of embeddable GIS components for developers to build custom applications. Using ArcGIS Engine, developers can incorporate ArcGIS functions into applications such as Microsoft Word and Excel as well as into custom applications that deliver focused GIS solutions to many users.

ArcGIS Engine runs on Windows, UNIX, and Linux desktops and supports a range of application development environments, such as Visual Basic 6, Microsoft Visual Studio .NET, and numerous Java developer environments including ECLIPSE® and JBuilder™.

There are two parts to ArcGIS Engine:

- ArcGIS Engine Developer Kit is used by developers to build custom applications.

- ArcGIS Engine Runtime is for end users to enable their computers to run applications containing ArcGIS Engine components.

ArcGIS Engine Developer Kit is available as a standalone developer product and also as a key part of the EDN program. For more information on EDN, see Chapter 6, 'ESRI Developer Network'.

ArcGIS Engine Runtime deployments are sold as separate runtime licenses for each software seat. ArcGIS Desktop is enabled to run ArcGIS Engine Runtime applications so users of ArcView, ArcEditor, and ArcInfo can run applications built with ArcGIS Engine. Other users who want to run ArcGIS Engine Runtime applications must purchase and install the ArcGIS Engine Runtime software.

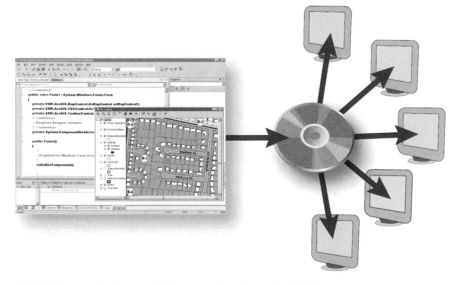

ArcGIS Engine is used by developers to build custom applications that can be deployed on many seats.

ArcGIS ENGINE DEVELOPER KIT

ArcGIS Engine includes a developer kit for building custom applications. Programmers install ArcGIS Engine Developer Kit on their computer and use it with their chosen programming language and development environment. ArcGIS Engine adds controls, tools, toolbars, and object libraries to the development environment for embedding GIS functions in applications. For example, a programmer can build a custom application that contains a map authored with ArcMap, some map tools from ArcGIS Engine, and other custom functions.

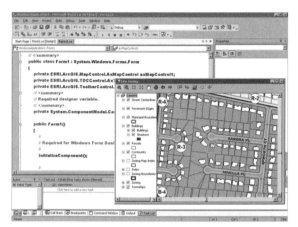

Shown above is an example of a custom ArcGIS Engine application being developed with VB. A map control, a table of contents control, a menu, and a toolbar have been added to this VB form. The map control is associated with an ArcMap document (a .mxd file) used to draw and query interactive maps.

Open support for programming languages and frameworks

In addition to supporting the COM environment, ArcGIS Engine also provides support for C++, .NET, and Java, enabling developers to work with ArcGIS Engine in their chosen developer framework across a range of computer operating systems.

Windows	UNIX and Linux
C++	C++
Java	Java
COM	
.NET	

ArcGIS Engine supports a number of computer platforms and programming languages.

Parts of ArcGIS Engine Developer Kit

ArcGIS Engine Developer Kit includes three key collections of GIS logic:

* Controls

* Toolbars and tools

* Object libraries

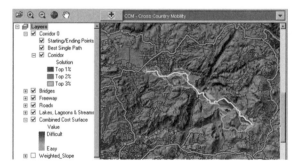

Example of an ArcGIS Engine application, including controls, toolbars, and objects

Controls

Controls are user interface components for ArcGIS that can be embedded and used in applications. For example, a map control and a table of contents control can be added to a custom application to present and use interactive maps.

Toolbars and tools

Toolbars contain collections of GIS tools for interacting with maps and geographic information in an application. Examples of tools used for interacting with maps include Pan, Zoom, Identify, and Selection. Tools are presented in the application interface using toolbars.

The process of building custom applications is simplified by having access to a rich set of commonly used tools and toolbars. Developers can simply drag-and-drop selected tools into custom applications or create their own custom tools for interacting with the map.

Object libraries

Object libraries are logical collections of programmable ArcObjects components, ranging from a geometry library to mapping, GIS data sources, and geodatabase libraries. Programmers use these libraries in their integrated development environments on Windows, UNIX, and Linux platforms to develop custom application code from simple to advanced. These same full GIS libraries form the basis of ArcGIS Desktop and ArcGIS Server.

These ArcObjects libraries support all the comprehensive ArcGIS functions for developers and can be accessed through most commonly used development environments—for example, Visual Basic 6, Delphi, C++, Java, Visual Basic .NET, and C#.

Example of the Map Navigation toolbar holding interactive tools for Zoom, Pan, Full Extent, and Previous Extent

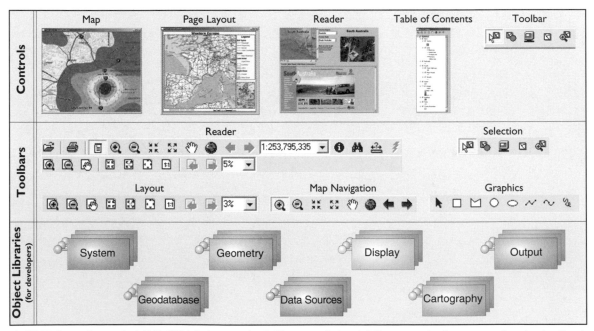

ArcGIS Engine contains sets of embeddable GIS logic that are used to build custom applications, including some user interface components (controls and tools) and programmable object libraries.

ArcGIS Engine RUNTIME EXTENSIONS

ArcGIS Engine Runtime has four optional extensions that enable additional application programming capabilities. The functions supported by these extensions are similar to ArcGIS Desktop extensions in that they must be enabled on each ArcGIS Engine Runtime seat.

Spatial

The Spatial extension adds comprehensive raster geoprocessing functions to the ArcGIS Engine Runtime environment. These additional capabilities are accessed via the Spatial Analyst object library.

3D

The 3D extension adds 3D analysis and display functions to the ArcGIS Engine Runtime environment. Additional capabilities include Scene and Globe developer controls and tools, as well as a set of 3D object libraries for Scene and Globe.

Geodatabase Update

The Geodatabase Update extension adds the ability to write to and update any geodatabase using ArcGIS Engine applications. This is used to build custom GIS editing applications. These additional capabilities are accessed via an enterprise geodatabase object library.

Network

The Network extension provides a complete set of embeddable network analysis and modeling functions to ArcGIS Engine Runtime.

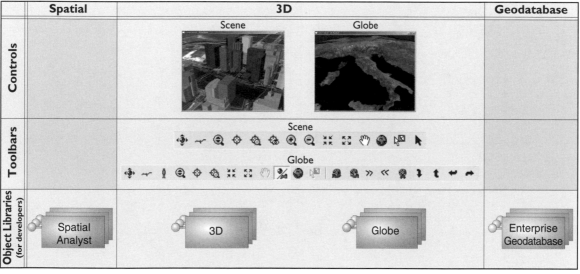

An overview of some of the developer components in the ArcGIS Engine optional extensions.

DEVELOPING APPLICATIONS WITH ArcGIS ENGINE

Developers build ArcGIS Engine applications in their chosen integrated development environment (IDE), such as:

- Microsoft Visual Studio or Delphi™ for Windows developers

- ECLIPSE, Sun ONE Studio™, or Borland® JBuilder for Java developers

Developers register the ArcGIS Engine Developer components with their IDE, then create a forms-based application, adding in ArcGIS Engine components and writing code to build their application.

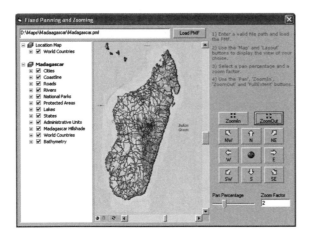

For example, a Java developer can build a focused GIS mapping application by adding a map control, a table of contents control, and selected toolbars to his or her application. The developer can associate an ArcMap .mxd file with the map control and program additional buttons and other functions for focused tasks. The finished application can then be deployed to many users.

Deploying ArcGIS Engine applications

Once built, ArcGIS Engine applications can be installed on two types of ArcGIS seats:

- ArcGIS Engine Runtime seats that are enabled to run ArcGIS Engine applications

- Existing ArcGIS Desktop seats (that is, seats running ArcView, ArcEditor, or ArcInfo) that are equipped to run ArcGIS Engine applications

An ArcGIS Engine Runtime installation CD–ROM is included with the ArcGIS Engine Developer Kit Media Kit and can be installed and configured on many computers. An authorization file is required to enable ArcGIS Engine capabilities on each computer. The Runtime extensions to ArcGIS Engine can also be enabled by adding a line to the authorization file.

HOW IS ArcGIS Engine USED?

ArcGIS Engine is used to build a wide range of GIS applications and for embedding GIS into any application. Some GIS departments want to build focused GIS viewers with tools relevant for their end users. In other scenarios, just a piece of GIS is combined with other information tools for performing key tasks and work flows.

For example, a city government department may want to build a series of focused parcel review applications that access information from the GIS database, integrating it with critical enterprise work orders for permitting, taxation, planning review, and so forth.

ArcGIS Engine development environment

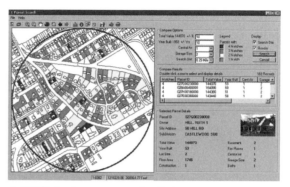

ArcGIS Engine city government parcel application

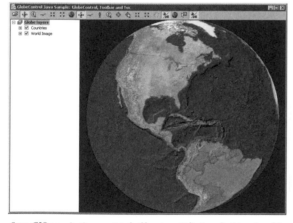

Some GIS organizations want to build custom applications for interactive globe viewing with the ArcGIS Engine 3D extension.

ArcGIS Engine components can be embedded in Microsoft Word documents and Microsoft Excel spreadsheets.

WHY USE ArcGIS Engine?

Many users require focused, lightweight access to GIS embedded in an application or as a standalone application. For example, users may need much less than ArcView yet still require access to sophisticated GIS logic in their application. In cases where users need focused, customized access to GIS, ArcGIS Engine provides a lower-cost, lightweight option.

ArcGIS Engine is used to:

• Embed GIS logic in custom applications.

• Efficiently build and deploy GIS applications.

• Provide access to advanced GIS logic from simple applications.

• Embed GIS logic and maps in other applications.

• Build cross platform applications with C++ or Java.

6

ESRI Developer Network

The ESRI Developer Network (EDN) represents a community of software developers who build and deploy applications with ArcGIS.

The goals of EDN are to:

- Provide a complete system for GIS developers building on the ESRI platform.

- Make ESRI developer technology easily available and affordable for developers through a single developer product.

- Foster and support a vital GIS developer community.

EDN is available to all kinds of developers including commercial developers, consultants, systems integrators, and end use developers.

GIS developers can obtain the complete ArcGIS Software Developer Kit by subscribing to EDN. Each subscription covers the right to develop with ESRI software for 12 months and is renewable each year.

The EDN annual subscription includes the EDN software library for the following products and developer resources, which can be used for creating a wide range of custom GIS applications and solutions:

- ArcGIS Engine

- ArcGIS Server

- ArcIMS

- ArcSDE

- ArcWeb Services (100,000 development credits)

The EDN subscription includes the ability to use any of these products for building, testing, and demonstrating custom applications. To deploy these applications, GIS end users need to buy appropriate software licenses for deploying underlying ArcGIS software.

Technical support and instructor-led training for developers is optionally available as part of an EDN subscription. These options provide developers access to the developer support hot line, e-mail, and other technical support for dealing with developer issues.

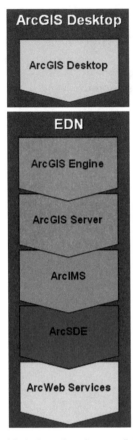

EDN is designed for developers who need access to all ArcGIS technology for application development.

There are three primary components necessary to begin development with the EDN software library. First, ArcGIS Desktop (ArcView, ArcEditor, or ArcInfo) is needed. ArcGIS Desktop is used to author geographic information elements such as datasets, maps, layers, geoprocessing models, and 3D globe projects that can be leveraged and embedded into custom applications using EDN. ArcGIS Desktop also provides the runtime environment for testing and demonstrating desktop applications and extensions.

Next, an annual subscription to the EDN program is required, which includes access to developer technology and resources for ArcGIS.

Finally, developers will need to determine what type of developer technical support they want. One option is to purchase direct phone support as part of EDN. Or the EDN Web site can be used to obtain developer help and support. Instructor-led training courses and technical support for EDN are also available.

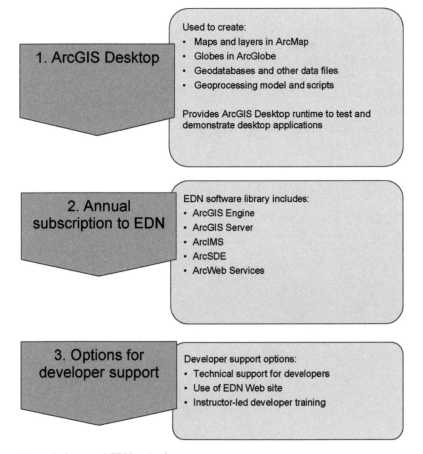

Effective development with EDN involves three components.

A companion Web site at *http://edn.esri.com* provides ongoing developer support and resources. The EDN Web site is a major component of the EDN program for supporting the ArcGIS developer community. It provides access to in-depth developer information such as code samples, technical articles, Webcasts, and e-mail alerts for subscribers. EDN developers can help one another by participating in developer forums and by sharing and reusing code from other developers in the EDN community.

Additional capabilities of the EDN Web site include the ability to download software updates, preview releases for developers, and receive invitations to special events for developers.

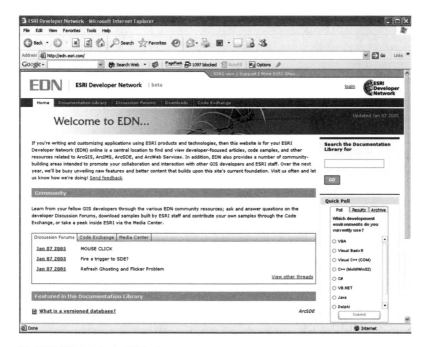

The EDN Web site is for ArcGIS developers.

The heart of ArcGIS is built and extended using the ArcObjects software component library. ArcObjects is an integrated collection of cross platform GIS software components that are client and server ready.

This shared library of ArcObjects provides a common developer experience across ArcGIS Desktop, ArcGIS Engine, and ArcGIS Server. It is built using a modular, scalable, cross platform architecture and offers a series of standard APIs for C++, .NET, and Java developers. ArcGIS provides a set of deployment options and resources for EDN developers.

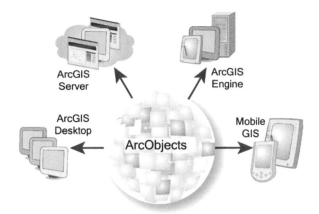

ArcObjects can be deployed in a number of frameworks. EDN provides the developer resources for all of these.

EDN includes the ability to develop with all ArcGIS capabilities. Once an ArcGIS Desktop seat and an EDN subscription have been acquired, developers have access to the following capabilities:

ARcGIS DESKTOP

ArcGIS Desktop (ArcView, ArcEditor, and ArcInfo) can be customized with easy-to-use, drag-and-drop menu-driven tools or by using its extensible object model. Customizations can range from a simple command to a complex application extension. These represent the same methods that ESRI development teams use to build ArcGIS Desktop and its extensions.

Microsoft Visual Basic for Applications (VBA) and the ArcGIS Desktop Software Developer Kit are included with ArcGIS Desktop for scripting and application customization. Both .NET and COM APIs can be used to customize and extend ArcGIS Desktop.

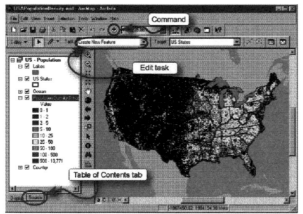

ArcMap interface illustrating some examples of how custom code and tools can be plugged into ArcGIS Desktop

ARcGIS SERVER

ArcGIS Server provides developers with the ability to build advanced GIS services and Web applications in a server environment. Developers use ArcGIS Server to deliver advanced GIS functionality to a wide range of users. ArcGIS Server is built from the same modular, scalable, and cross platform ArcObjects components that comprise the ArcGIS system.

Development technology for ArcGIS Server includes a number of key parts for building comprehensive server-based applications. This includes support for:

* .NET and J2EE enterprise framework

* Services-oriented architectures (SOAs)

* Central Web applications using .NET ASP and Java JSP

* Web application templates, Web controls, and tools for building Web applications

* SOAP-based Web services and other message-based interfaces

* Out-of-the-box and custom-built GIS server objects

Example of a Web application built using application templates and Web controls included in the ArcGIS Server ADF.

ArcGIS ENGINE

ArcGIS Engine is a core set of cross platform ArcObjects components compatible with multiple APIs such as .NET, Java, COM, and C++. Developers can use these embeddable components to build custom GIS and mapping applications. ArcGIS Engine applications can be built and deployed on Microsoft Windows, Sun Solaris, and Linux platforms. The applications can vary from simple map viewers to custom GIS editing programs.

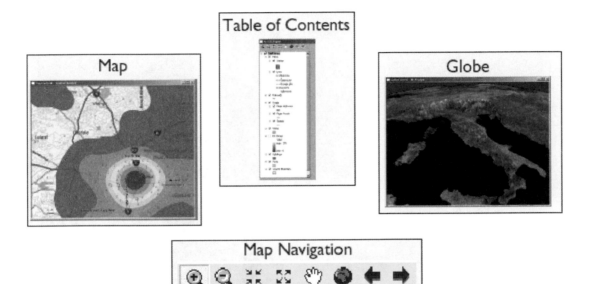

ArcGIS Engine includes a number of user interface controls and tools (in addition to the ArcObjects software libraries) for custom application development.

ArcSDE

ArcSDE is an advanced spatial data server, providing a gateway for storing, managing, and using geographic data in a number of widely used DBMSs for multiple client applications.

ArcSDE provides a number of options for building applications that work with and query information contained in multiuser geodatabases. In addition to the use of the ArcObjects component library provided with the other developer kits, the ArcSDE Developer Kit includes a robust C API and a comparable Java API. In addition, if IBM DB2 Spatial Extender or Informix Spatial DataBlade is used, a number of SQL functions for the spatial types are available and are documented as part of the ArcSDE developer content.

Here is an example of use of SQL for performing combined spatial and attribute queries:

```
select sa.name "Sensitive Facilities",
hs.name "Hazardous Sites"

from sensitive_facilities sf,
hazardous_sites hs

where ST_Overlaps (sf.zone, ST_Buffer
(hs.location,(5 * 5280))) = 't';
```

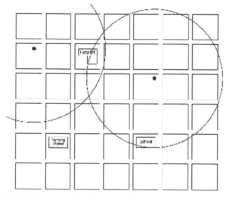

This SQL query selects the sensitive facilities that lie within a five-mile buffer radius of hazardous site locations.

ArcIMS

ArcIMS developers work with ArcXML, the openly published communication protocol and Web API for ArcIMS, as well as a series of Internet connector technologies for building Web applications accessed through Web browsers. ArcIMS connector technologies for developers include ActiveX, .NET, Java, and ColdFusion.

ArcXML is the message protocol for communicating with ArcIMS. ArcXML is implemented as a series of requests and responses for interacting with an ArcIMS server, which provides the functional ArcIMS capabilities for serving maps and data in the appropriate format and sending these to the client.

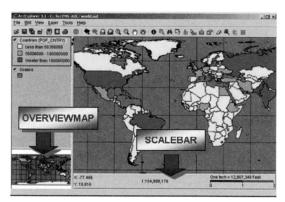

ArcIMS developers build custom Web applications using HTML, Java, ColdFusion, or .NET tools. ArcXML is also used to write scripts for ArcIMS services to serve maps, datasets, map elements, and so on.

ArcWEB SERVICES

ArcWeb Services provide Web service access to both GIS data content and GIS functions that work in concert with the data services—on demand when needed. This eliminates the overhead of purchasing and maintaining large datasets and provides useful content that developers can embed and consume in Web-based GIS applications and solutions. ArcWeb Services are always available on the Web so that users with strong Internet support can plug in to these services and use them at any time.

General access to ArcWeb Services is sold commercially as a series of credits (in blocks of 100,000 credits). Each time users access ArcWeb Services, they spend a portion of their credits. Each EDN subscription includes one block of 100,000 credits for use in application development, testing, and demonstration.

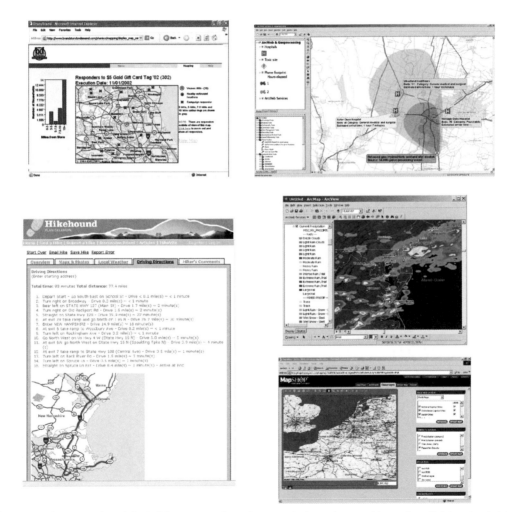

ArcWeb Services provide access to terabytes of data including street maps, live weather maps, orthophotography, topographic maps, live traffic information, shaded relief imagery, flood data, and census data. These Web services for data delivery also include focused tools that work with each data source. For example, users can perform routing, place finding, address geocoding, proximity searches, queries, analyses, and reporting. The content is provided by a number of key companies that include Tele Atlas, Meteorlogix, GlobeXplorer, Pixxures, AND, National Geographic, ESRI BIS, and TrafficCast.

TYPES OF DEVELOPMENT PROJECTS PERFORMED WITH EDN

EDN provides a complete system for developing desktop and server applications as well as for embedding GIS logic in other applications. This allows developers to:

- Embed GIS maps and functionality in other applications.

- Build and deploy custom applications.

- Build custom extensions and tools for ArcGIS Desktop (ArcView, ArcEditor, and ArcInfo).

- Extend the ArcGIS architecture and data model.

- Build Web services and applications with ArcGIS Desktop.

7

Mobile GIS using ArcPad and ArcGIS

Mobile computing is creating fundamental changes by adding the ability to take GIS with you into the field and interact directly with the world around you. Mobile GIS comprises the integration of a number of technologies:

- GIS

- Mobile hardware in the form of lightweight devices and ruggedized field PCs

- GPS

- Wireless communications for Internet GIS access

Traditionally, the process of field data collection and editing has been time-consuming and error prone. Geographic data traveled into the field in the form of paper maps. Field edits were performed using sketches and notes on paper maps and clipboards. Once back in the office, these field edits were deciphered and manually entered into the GIS database. The result has been that GIS data has often not been as up-to-date or as accurate as it should have been. Consequently, GIS analysis and decisions have been delayed.

Recent developments in mobile technologies have enabled GIS information to be taken into the field as digital maps on compact, powerful, mobile computers, providing field access to enterprise geographic information. This enables organizations to add real-time (and near real-time) information to their enterprise database and applications, speeding up analysis, display, and decision making by using up-to-date, more accurate spatial data.

Many field-based tasks utilize geographic information that has benefited from the increased efficiency and accuracy of mobile GIS, including:

- Asset inventory, which usually requires field data collection or mapping

- Asset maintenance, which usually requires updates to attribute information and geometry of GIS features

- Inspections, typically involving field assets or legal code compliance

- Incident reporting—for example, spatially recording accidents or events

- GIS analysis and decision making

These field-based tasks are common to many GIS applications, such as utility inspections and maintenance, mapping of natural resources, mineral exploration, recording of accidents, inspection of compliance to local government codes, mapping of wildfires, and many more.

Some of the field-based tasks involve fairly simple operations that require simple geographic tools. In contrast, some field-based tasks involve complex operations and, consequently, require sophisticated geographic tools. ArcGIS includes applications that meet the requirements of both of these needs:

- ArcPad focuses on field tasks that require relatively simple geographic tools. These tasks are typically performed on handheld computers (running Microsoft Windows CE or Pocket PC).

- ArcGIS Desktop and ArcGIS Engine focus on field tasks that require more sophisticated geographic tools. These tasks are typically performed on high-end Tablet PCs.

Field GIS also relies heavily on application customization to simplify mobile work tasks as well as wireless access to real-time data feeds from central GIS Web servers, such as sites deployed with ArcIMS and ArcGIS Server.

ESRI's ArcPad software is mobile mapping and GIS technology for mobile Windows devices. ArcPad provides database access, mapping, GIS, and GPS integration to field users via handheld and mobile devices. Data collection with ArcPad is fast and easy and improves field-based data validation and availability.

COMMON ArcPad FUNCTIONS

- Support for industry-standard vector and raster image display

- ArcIMS client for data access via wireless technology

- Map navigation, including pan and zoom, spatial bookmarks, and center on the current GPS position

- Data query to identify features, display hyperlinks, and locate features

- Map measurement: distance, area, and bearings

- GPS navigation to connect a GPS and let ArcPad guide you

- Simple editing: creating and editing spatial data using input from the mouse pointer, pen, or GPS

- Mobile geodatabase editing: checking out, converting, and projecting GIS data using ArcGIS; editing in the field with ArcPad, and posting changes back to the central GIS database

- Application development to automate GIS fieldwork

EXAMPLES OF ArcPad APPLICATIONS

ArcPad is typically used for building specialized mapping and data collection applications. The following list includes examples of ArcPad applications:

- Street sign inventory
- Power pole maintenance
- Meter reading
- Road pavement management
- Military fieldwork
- Mineral exploration
- Habitat studies
- Toxic inventory
- Crop management
- Property damage assessment
- Field surveying
- Incident reporting and inspection
- Real-time wildfire boundary mapping
- Refuse container inventory
- Wildlife tracking
- GIS data validation

ArcPad APPLICATION BUILDER

Creating a personalized and custom field solution for mapping, data collection, and updates is essential for mobile GIS. ArcPad users are able to customize ArcPad and build focused applications using ArcPad Application Builder.

ArcPad Application Builder runs on Windows computers. Developers build custom applications within this environment and can deploy them on numerous ArcPad devices in their organization.

ArcPad supports numerous Windows CE and Pocket PC devices.

Many users have requirements for high-end field computers with built-in GPS. These field computers run the full Windows operating system and are used for remotely performing many advanced, computer-based tasks. In recent years, Microsoft has introduced a new operating system, Microsoft Windows XP Tablet PC Edition, which enables many innovative features such as pen-based computing, digital ink technology, and enhanced mobility functions.

ArcGIS Desktop running on Tablet PCs is a powerful mobile platform for advanced GIS field computing. Tablet PC technology enables users to redline designs, capture accurate field measurements using GPS, and leverage the comprehensive functionality of ArcGIS and the geodatabase in the field.

OVERVIEW OF TABLET PC

A key capability of the Tablet PC is the use of a pen-based interface for computer interaction, sketching, and capturing notes. These activities are based on a technology called digital ink. Digital ink is created through sketching and can be converted to text using the text recognition engine, added to the edit sketch for any editing task, or stored as a graphic in datasets.

The Tablet PC platform is commonly used in four ways:

- Tablet PC as a notebook computer: The Windows XP Tablet PC Edition is a superset of the existing Windows XP operating system.

- Tablet PC pen-based technology: The Tablet PC lets you drive the Windows XP operating system and all Windows-based applications using a digital pen instead of a mouse. For example, in ArcGIS, the digital pen can be used to push buttons on toolbars and draw on the map.

- Windows XP speech recognition: The speech recognition functionality is embedded within the Tablet PC input panel and can be used with ArcGIS for dictation functions.

- Tablet PC digital ink technology: Pen interfaces are used for sketching with Tablet PCs. Digital ink, created through sketching, can be converted to text using the text recognition engine, added to the edit sketch for completion of a current editing task, or stored as a graphic.

ArcGIS Desktop TABLET TOOLS

ArcGIS includes a series of tools for Tablet PCs that enable users to take advantage of its innovative features—pen-based computing, digital ink technology, and enhanced mobility functions as well as the rich mapping and data compilation capabilities of ArcGIS.

The primary focus at ArcGIS 9 has been on supporting ArcGIS Desktop and its rich mapping and editing tools on Tablet PCs. Tablet PC capabilities also work well with ArcGIS Engine. For example, ArcGIS Engine users can use the pen interface to highlight and query features, add and change attribute values, and interact with their custom applications.

The ArcGIS Desktop application ArcMap has been extended with a Tablet PC toolbar that integrates digital ink technology with ArcGIS. Using the Tablet toolbar, users can access the ink tools to create notes or sketch diagrams and tie them to a geographic location. The ink tools can also be used to highlight features on a map and sketch shapes that can be used to perform GIS editing tasks. Tablet tools make use of ink technology such as gestures and text recognition.

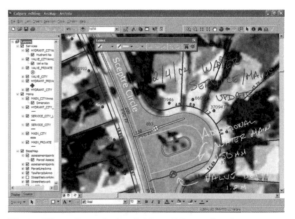

The ArcGIS mapping application ArcMap includes a toolbar that integrates digital ink technology with ArcGIS. Using the Tablet toolbar, you can access the Pen tool to create notes or sketch diagrams and tie them to a geographic location.

The Tablet tools for ArcGIS Desktop add a graphic element called an ink graphic. Ink graphics are stored along with other graphic elements and text in the map's graphics layer or as annotation in the geodatabase. Users can create an ink graphic using ArcGIS and choose whether to store it in the map or the geodatabase being edited.

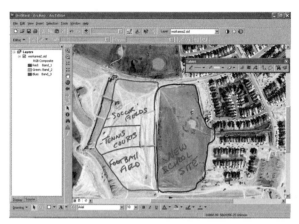

Sketches and notes created in ArcMap on the Tablet PC are geographically referenced and can be saved as map graphics or as annotation in the geodatabase.

Here is a list of some of the Tablet toolbar functions:

- Pen tool—Creates new ink graphics on the map.

- Highlighter tool—Draws transparent ink on the map for highlighting features.

- Erase tool—Removes strokes of ink from the map display.

- Finish Ink Sketch command—Creates new ink graphic elements from the ink that is being collected on the map.

- Clear Ink Sketch command—Removes all ink that is being collected.

- Add Ink To Sketch command—Allows ink to be used to complete the current editing task (such as creating new features).

- Recognize Ink Graphic command—Converts selected ink graphics written with the Pen tool to text elements.

- Reactivate the Selected Ink Graphic command— Creates a new ink sketch from the selected ink graphic so it can be edited using the Pen or Highlighter tool.

- Find Ink Graphic tool—searches the map or a geodatabase for ink based on its recognized text.

TABLET PC CUSTOMIZATION

Mobile GIS requires focused application designs and customization to build productive, simple user interfaces for field-workers. Since ArcGIS is being used, the same customization and ArcObjects programming work done for all of ArcGIS can be leveraged for building and deploying Tablet PC applications.

8 GIS data concepts and the geodatabase

A cornerstone of ArcGIS is its ability to access GIS data in any format and use multiple databases and file-based datasets concurrently.

ArcGIS has a high-level generic information model for representing geographic information, such as features, rasters, and other spatial data types. ArcGIS supports an implementation of the data model for both file systems and DBMSs.

Support for file-based models includes access to numerous GIS datasets such as coverages, shapefiles, grids, images, and TINs. The geodatabase model manages the same types of geographic information in relational databases, providing many of the data management benefits offered by a DBMS.

File-based datasets
Coverages
Shapefiles
Grids
TINs
Images (numerous formats)
Vector Product Format (VPF) files
CAD files (numerous formats)
Tables (numerous formats)

Geodatabases
Oracle
Oracle with Spatial or Locator
DB2 with its Spatial Type
Informix with its Spatial Type
SQL Server
Personal Geodatabases (Microsoft Access)

Some of the common GIS data formats that can be used directly in ArcGIS. Access to and from numerous additional formats is supported through data conversion and interoperability extensions. GIS data is also accessible through the Web using various XML and Web schemas, such as Geodatabase XML, ArcXML, SOAP, WMS; and OGC specifications, such as GML and WFS.

Both the file-based datasets and the DBMS-based datasets define a generic model for geographic information. This generic model can be used to define and work with a wide variety of GIS applications. By defining and implementing the behavior of a generic geographic data model, geographic information in ArcGIS can be multipurpose, sharable, and standards-based. Most important, a comprehensive series of tools are available to work with the generic data types. Thus, ArcGIS provides a robust platform for virtually any GIS application.

ArcGIS Data Interoperability is an optional extension that adds critical support for working with data in virtually any spatial data format. The ArcGIS Data Interoperability extension was built in cooperation with Safe Software Inc. using their rich FME product. It provides tools to directly read, transform, and work in ArcGIS with many data formats, such as various advanced CAD data structures, GML, MapInfo files, and Intergraph GeoMedia warehouses. It also supports the export of spatial data into numerous industry formats.

The geodatabase has three key aspects:

- It is a comprehensive information model and a transaction model for GIS.

- It is the common application logic used in ArcGIS for accessing and working with all geographic data files and formats

- It is a physical instance of a collection of datasets stored in a file system or DBMS.

Users usually think of geodatabases as physical instances of information collections—primarily using a DBMS.

Geodatabases work across a range of DBMS architectures and file systems, come in many sizes, and have varying numbers of users. They can scale from small, single-user databases built on files up to larger work group, department, and enterprise databases accessed by many users. Two types of geodatabase architectures are available: personal geodatabases and multiuser geodatabases.

Personal geodatabases, which are freely available to all ArcGIS users, use the Microsoft Jet Engine database file structure to persist GIS data in smaller databases. Personal geodatabases are much like file-based folders and hold databases up to 2 GB in size. Microsoft Access is used to work with attribute tables in personal geodatabases.

Personal geodatabases are ideal for working with smaller datasets for GIS projects and in small work groups. Typically, users will employ multiple personal geodatabases for their data collections and access these simultaneously for their GIS work. Personal geodatabases support single-user editing. No versioning support is provided.

Multiuser geodatabases require the use of ArcSDE and work with a variety of DBMS storage models (IBM DB2, Informix, Oracle, and SQL Server). Multiuser geodatabases are primarily used in a wide range of work groups, departments, and enterprise settings. They take full advantage of their underlying DBMS architectures to support:

- Extremely large, continuous GIS databases

- Many simultaneous users

- Long transactions and versioned work flows

Multiuser geodatabases readily scale to extremely large sizes and numbers of users. Through many large geodatabase implementations, it has been found that DBMSs are efficient at moving the type of large binary objects required for GIS data in and out of tables. In addition, GIS database sizes and the number of supported users can be much larger than GIS file bases.

Geodatabase type	DBMS	Notes
Personal geodatabase	Microsoft Jet Engine (Access)	· Single-user editing · 2 GB size limit · No versioning support
Multiuser, versioned geodatabase	· Oracle · Oracle with Spatial or Locator · IBM DB2 · IBM Informix · Microsoft SQL Server	· Requires ArcSDE Gateway · Multiuser editing · Version-based work flows · Database size and number of users up to RDBMS limits

Summary of personal and multiuser geodatabases

GIS DATABASE REQUIREMENTS

- Scale to large sizes (multiple terabytes)

- Scale to large number of users (hundreds to thousands)

- Provide advanced GIS data models and behavior

- Maintain spatial data integrity

- Support multiple users

- Deliver fast data retrieval

- Use simple data structures such as OGC/ISO simple features

- Support long transactions and GIS work flows

- Support multiple uses and applications

- Proven to work through real case studies

Vector features (geographic objects with vector geometry) are a versatile and frequently used geographic data type, well suited for representing features with discrete boundaries, such as wells, streets, rivers, states, and parcels. A feature is simply an object that stores its geographic representation as one of its properties (or fields) in the row. Typically, features are spatially represented as points, lines, polygons, or annotation and are organized into feature classes. Three-dimensional features can also be represented using multipatch geometries.

Feature classes are collections of features of the same type with a common spatial representation and set of attributes stored in a database table—for example, a line feature class for roads.

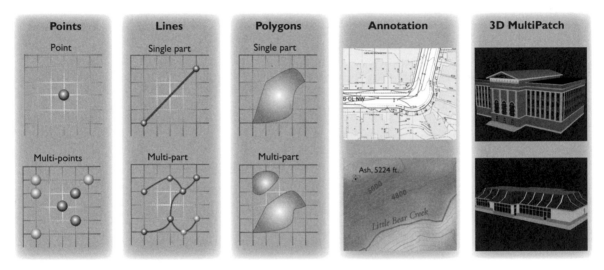

Common vector feature representations. Feature coordinates can be xy, xyz, or xyzm. Boundaries between coordinates can be straight line segments or curves. Multipatch geometries represent the outer shell of 3D shapes and can have image textures assigned for display.

Rasters are used to represent continuous layers, such as elevation, slope and aspect, vegetation, temperature, rainfall, plume dispersion, and so on. Rasters are most commonly used for the storage of aerial photographs and imagery of various kinds.

In addition to vector features and raster datasets, all other spatial data types can be managed and stored in the relational tables, allowing users the opportunity to manage all geographic data in a DBMS.

Raster datasets are the storage mechanisms for imagery data.

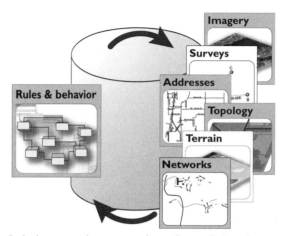

Geodatabases are used to manage and store diverse collections of geographic information types.

The geodatabase architecture is based on a series of simple yet essential database concepts. The DBMS provides a simple, formal data model for storing and working with information in tables. Users tend to think of the DBMS as inherently open because the simplicity and flexibility of the generic relational data model enable it to support a broad array of applications. Key DBMS concepts include:

- Data is organized into tables.

- Tables contain rows.

- All rows in a table have the same columns.

- Each column has a type, such as integer, decimal number, character, date, and so on.

- Relationships are used to associate rows from one table with rows in another table. This is based on a common column in each table, the primary key or the foreign key.

- Relational integrity rules exist for table-based datasets. For example, each row always shares the same columns, a domain lists the valid values or value ranges for a column, and so on.

- SQL, a series of relational functions and operators, is available to operate on the tables and their data elements.

- The SQL operators are designed to work with the generic relational data types, such as integers, decimal numbers, dates, and characters.

Feature class table

Shape	ID	PIN	Area	Addr	Code
	1	334-1626-001	7,342	341 Cherry Ct.	SFR
	2	334-1626-002	8,020	343 Cherry Ct.	UND
	3	334-1626-003	10,031	345 Cherry Ct.	SFR
	4	334-1626-004	9,254	347 Cherry Ct.	SFR
	5	334-1626-005	8,856	348 Cherry Ct.	UND
	6	334-1626-006	9,975	346 Cherry Ct.	SFR
	7	334-1626-007	8,230	344 Cherry Ct.	SFR
	8	334-1626-008	8,645	342 Cherry Ct.	SFR

Related ownership table

PIN	Owner	Acq.Date	Assessed	TaxStat
334-1626-001	G. Hall	1995/10/20	$115,500.00	02
334-1626-002	H. L Holmes	1993/10/06	$24,375.00	01
334-1626-003	W. Rodgers	1980/09/24	$175,500.00	02
334-1626-004	J. Williamson	1974/09/20	$135,750.00	02
334-1626-005	P. Goodman	1966/06/06	$30,350.00	02
334-1626-006	K. Staley	1942/10/24	$120,750.00	02
334-1626-007	J. Dormandy	1996/01/27	$110,650.00	01
334-1626-008	S. Gooley	2000/05/31	$145,750.00	02

Spatial tables in the geodatabase, such as feature classes and raster tables, adhere to these same DBMS principles. One of the columns holds the spatial data for each geographic object—for example, the shape field holds a polygon shape in a feature class table. Various column types in each DBMS are used to hold the shape field in the table. These are typically either a binary large object (BLOB) type or an extended spatial type that is supported in some DBMSs. For example, Oracle, with its Spatial extension, provides a spatial column type.

SQL operates on the rows, columns, and types in tables. The column types (the numbers, characters, dates, BLOBs, spatial types, and so on) are objects in the SQL algebra.

The DBMS manages these simple data types and tables, while additional application logic implements more complex object behavior and integrity constraints. Developers wanting to implement higher-level objects with behavior and logic write application code to do so.

For example, an organization may implement a table named EMPLOYEES as follows:

Name (Last)	Name (First)	DOH	Salary
Crosier	James	10-10-98	10,000.75
Clark	Rosemary	03-12-95	55,000.50
Brown	Pete	06-12-89	23,000.00

A simple relational data table containing rows and columns. The data in each column adheres to a particular data type, such as character, date, and number.

The business objects being modeled for the employees and their names, salaries, and hire dates are not implemented as relational objects. More sophisticated and focused application logic is required to implement behavior and integrity on these business objects. Examples of logic that could be implemented to support employment activities are hiring, implementing a pay raise, employee resignations, promotions, and managing benefits.

Similar business objects are universally applied in GIS. For example, feature classes, map layers, topologies, networks, linear referencing systems, raster catalogs, dimensions, annotations, terrains, and so forth are all examples of advanced objects used to implement GIS behavior on top of the simple spatial representations stored in the DBMS.

Tables with spatial columns are not enough for GIS applications. Both sets of objects (the simple DBMS relational column types and the application objects) are necessary for building information systems. It is important to emphasize the concept that higher-level objects are universally used in DBMS applications using application logic.

WHERE DOES THE APPLICATION LOGIC BELONG?

Various alternatives exist. Users can persist this higher-level logic in a number of ways. For example, the logic could be implemented as:

• Stored procedures and database triggers in the DBMS

• Extended types in the DBMS

• A separate application tier that works on the rows and column types in tables

Countless DBMS implementations over the past two decades have demonstrated overwhelmingly that the use of an application tier is appropriate for advanced applications. For example, all the widely adopted customer information systems (CIS), enterprise resource planning (ERP) systems, and accounting packages implement advanced application logic in the application tier, which enables more openness and extensibility, higher performance, richer toolsets, and increased flexibility.

The geodatabase employs this same multitier application architecture by implementing advanced logic and behavior in the application tier on top of the DBMS for a series of generic GIS objects.

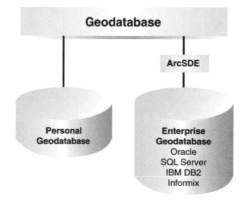

The geodatabase implements advanced logic and behavior in the application tier on top of the DBMS.

Responsibility for management of geographic datasets is shared between GIS software and generic DBMS software. Certain aspects of geographic dataset management, such as disk-based storage, definition of attribute types, associative query processing, and multiuser transaction processing, are delegated to the DBMS. The GIS application retains responsibility for defining the specific DBMS schema used to represent various geographic datasets and for domain-specific logic, which maintains the integrity and utility of the underlying records.

In effect, the DBMS is used as one of a series of implementation mechanisms for persisting geographic datasets. However, the DBMS does not fully define the semantics of the geographic data. This could be considered a multitier architecture (application and storage), where aspects related to data storage and retrieval are implemented in the storage (DBMS) tier as simple tables, while high-level data integrity and information processing functions are retained in the application and domain software (GIS).

The geodatabase is implemented using the same multitier application architecture found in other advanced DBMS applications. The geodatabase objects are persisted as rows in DBMS tables that have identity, and the behavior is supplied through the geodatabase application logic.

At the core of the geodatabase is a standard (that is, not exotic) relational database schema (a series of standard DBMS tables, column types, indexes, and so on). This simple physical storage works in concert with, and is controlled by, a set of higher-level application objects hosted in the application tier, which can be an ArcGIS client or an ArcGIS server. These geodatabase objects define a generic GIS information model that is shared by all ArcGIS applications and users. The purpose of the geodatabase objects is to expose a high-level GIS information model to clients and to persist the detailed implementation of this model in any appropriate storage model, for example, in standard DBMS tables, in file systems, and as XML streams.

All ArcGIS applications interact with this generic GIS object model for geodatabases, not with the actual SQL-based DBMS instance. The geodatabase software components implement behavior and integrity rules implicit in the generic model and translate data requests to the appropriate physical database design.

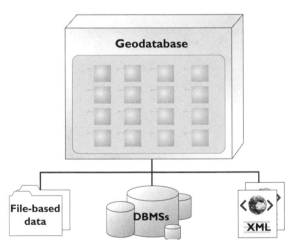

The separation of geodatabase logic from storage enables support for numerous file types, DBMSs, and XML.

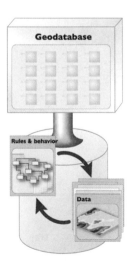

The geodatabase architecture is based on simple relational storage and comprehensive application logic.

Geodatabase storage includes both the schema and rule base for each geographic dataset plus simple, tabular storage of the spatial and attribute data.

The geodatabase schema includes the definitions, integrity rules, and behavior for each geographic dataset. These include properties for feature classes, topologies, networks, raster catalogs, relationships, domains, and so forth. The schema is persisted in a collection of geodatabase metatables in the DBMS that defines the integrity and behavior of the geographic information.

The spatial representations are most commonly stored as either vector features or as raster datasets along with traditional tabular attributes. For example, a DBMS table can be used to store a feature collection where each row in the table represents a feature. A shape column in each row is used to hold the geometry or shape of the feature. The shape column holding the geometry is typically one of two column types:

- A BLOB column type

- A spatial column type, if the DBMS supports it

A homogeneous collection of common features, each having the same spatial representation, such as a point, line, or polygon, and a common set of attribute columns, is referred to as a feature class and is managed in a single table.

Raster and imagery data types are managed and stored in relational tables as well. Raster data is typically much larger in size and requires a side table for storage. The raster is cut into smaller pieces, or blocks, and stored in individual rows in the separate block table.

The column types that hold the vector and raster geometry vary from database to database. When the DBMS supports spatial type extensions, the geodatabase can readily use them to hold the spatial geometry. ESRI was closely involved in efforts to extend SQL for spatial as the primary authors of the SQL 3 MM Spatial and the OGC Simple Features SQL specifications. ESRI has focused on support for these types, as well as the independent Oracle Spatial types, in the persistence of geodatabases using DBMS standards.

Feature dataset
Contains spatially-related feature classes with the topology and network objects that bind them. Feature classes in a feature dataset have spatial reference.

Feature class
A table with a shape field containing point, line, or polygon geometries for geographic features. Each row is a feature.

Table
A collection of rows, each containing the same fields. Feature classes are tables with shape fields.

Domain
Defines a set or range of valid values for a field.

Relationship class
Associates objects from a feature class or table to objects in another feature class or table. Relationship classes can optionally have user-defined fields.

Topology
Integrity rules that define the behavior of geographically integrated features.

Geometric network
Rules for managing connectivity among features in a set of feature classes.

Survey dataset
Contains survey measurements that are used to calculate coordinates linked to feature geometries in survey-aware feature classes.

Raster dataset
Contains rasters that represent continuous geographic phenomena.

Metadata document
An XML document that can be associated with every dataset. Commonly used in ArcIMS and other server applications.

Geoprocessing tools
A collection of data flow and work flow processes for performing data management, analysis, and modeling.

A geodatabase is a store of geographic data implemented with the relational database of your choice. All geodatabase elements are managed in standard DBMS tables using standard SQL data types. GIS application logic is used to implement integrity rules and GIS behavior on the simple relational structure. These are some of the structural elements of a geodatabase used to develop a rich, geographic information model.

Transactions are packages of work that make changes to databases. GIS databases, like other database applications, must support update transactions that enforce data integrity and application behavior. However, GIS users have some specialized transactional requirements, the most important of which is that transactions must span long periods of time (sometimes days and months, not just seconds or minutes).

Additionally, a single editing session in a GIS can involve changes to multiple rows in multiple tables. Users need to be able to undo and redo changes. Editing sessions can span several hours or even days. Often the edits must be performed in a system that is disconnected from the central, shared database.

Because GIS work flow processes may span days or months, the GIS database must remain continuously available for daily operations, where each user might have a personal view or state of the shared GIS database.

In a multiuser database, the GIS transactions must be orchestrated on the DBMS's short transaction framework. ArcSDE plays a key role during these operations by managing the high-level, complex GIS transactions on the simple DBMS transaction framework.

GIS users have many cases in which long transaction work flows are critical. In most instances, these are made possible through the use of a multiuser DBMS and ArcSDE to manage updates to the central GIS database.

The following are examples of GIS data compilation work flows that require a long transaction model:

- Multiple edit sessions—A single GIS database update may require numerous changes that span multiple edit sessions occurring over a few days or weeks.

- Multiuser editing—Multiple editors often need to concurrently update the same spatially integrated features. Each user needs to work with a personalized database state, viewing individual updates and ignoring updates by other editors. Eventually, each user needs to post and reconcile their updates with the other editors to identify and resolve any conflicts.

- Checkout/check-in transactions—It's often necessary to check out a portion of a database for a particular area or district to a personal computer and update that information in a disconnected session that could last

for days or weeks. Those updates must be posted to the main database. In other cases, a portion of a large geodatabase may be taken into the field for validation and update with field computers.

- History—Sometimes it's advantageous to maintain a historical version of each feature in a GIS database, even after that particular version has been updated, to maintain a copy of the retired and changed features in an archive or to track an individual feature's history—for example, parcel lineage or feature update properties in a national mapping database.

- Transfer of change-only updates—Data collection can be a collaborate effort that requires the sharing of updates across the Internet in a well-defined XML schema for sharing change-only updates between databases.

- Distributed geographic databases—A regional database may be a partial copy of a main corporate GIS database for a particular geographic region. Periodically, the two databases must be synchronized by exchanging updates.

- Loosely coupled replication across DBMSs—Often, GIS data must be synchronized among a series of database copies (replicas), where each site performs its own updates on its local database. Periodically, the updates must be transferred from each database replica to the others and their contents synchronized. Many times the DBMSs are different—for example, replicating datasets among SQL Server, Oracle, and IBM DB2.

WHAT IS VERSIONING?

The geodatabase mechanism for managing these and many other critical GIS work flows is to maintain multiple states in the geodatabase and, most important, do so while ensuring the integrity of the GIS database. This ability to manage, work with, and view multiple states is based on versioning. As the name implies, versioning explicitly records versions of individual features and objects as they are modified, added, and retired through various states. A version explicitly records each state of a feature or object as a row in a table along with important transaction information.

Versions explicitly record the object states of a geodatabase in two delta tables: the Adds table and the Deletes table. Simple queries are used to view and work with any desired state of the geodatabase—for example, to view the database state for a point in time or see a particular user's current version with edits.

ArcSDE plays a critical role in versioned geodatabase applications and is used to manage long transactions in each DBMS as well as across different systems.

Default Version
before editing

45	44
41	42	43

Base Table

ObjectID	Perimeter	Bldg_Code	Area
41	30106.25	04	1253459.45
42	27458.37	04	1048592.56
43	32945.09	04	1584562.04
44	30001.55	04	1116459.67
45	30556.38	04	1362965.03

Adds Table

ObjectID	Other Columns	State_ID

Deletes Table

Deleted_at	Deletes_Row_ID	State_ID

Updated Feature
after edit session

47	
	44
41	42	43

Base Table

ObjectID	Perimeter	Bldg_Code	Area
41	30106.25	04	1253459.45
42	27458.37	04	1048592.56
43	32945.09	04	1584562.04
44	30001.55	04	1116459.67
47	43834.07	06	1953473.02

Adds Table

ObjectID	Other Columns	State_ID
47	<....>	47

Deletes Table

Deleted_at	Deletes_Row_ID	State_ID
45	<....>	0

Versions explicitly record the object states of a geodatabase.

Geodatabase XML represents ESRI's open mechanism for information interchange between geodatabases and other external systems. ESRI openly publishes and maintains the complete geodatabase schema and content as an XML specification and provides sample implementations to illustrate how users can share data updates between heterogeneous systems.

XML interchange of geospatial information to and from the geodatabase is greatly simplified using the geodatabase XML specification. External applications can receive XML data streams including:

- Exchange of complete lossless datasets

- Interchange of simple feature sets (much like shapefile interchange)

- Exchange of change-only (delta) record sets using XML streams to pass updates and changes among geodatabases and other external data structures

- Exchange and sharing of full or partial geodatabase schemas between ArcGIS users

Glossary

3D multipatch

See multipatch.

address geocoding

See geocoding.

analysis

The process of identifying a question or issue to be addressed, modeling the issue, investigating model results, interpreting the results, and possibly making a recommendation.

annotation

In ArcGIS, text or graphics on a map that can be individually selected, positioned, and modified by the software user. The text may represent either feature attributes or supplementary information. Annotation may be manually entered by the user or generated from labels. Annotation is stored either in a map document as text or graphic elements, or in a geodatabase as a feature class.

ArcIMS

ESRI software that allows for centrally hosting and serving GIS maps, data, and mapping applications as Web services. The administrative framework allows users to author configuration files, publish services, design Web pages, and administer ArcIMS Spatial Servers. ArcIMS supports Windows, Linux, and UNIX platforms and is customizable on many levels.

ArcSDE

Server software that provides a gateway for storing, managing, and using spatial data in one of the following commercial database management systems: IBM DB2 UDB, IBM Informix, Microsoft SQL Server, and Oracle. Common ArcSDE client applications include ArcGIS Desktop, ArcGIS Server, and ArcIMS.

ArcToolbox

A user interface in ArcGIS used for accessing and organizing a collection of geoprocessing tools, models, and scripts. ArcToolbox and ModelBuilder are used in concert to perform geoprocessing.

attribute

1. Information about a geographic feature in a GIS, usually stored in a table and linked to the feature by a unique identifier. For example, attributes of a river might include its name, length, and average depth.

2. In raster datasets, information associated with each unique value of raster cells.

3. Cartographic information that specifies how features are displayed and labeled on a map; the cartographic attributes of a river might include line thickness, line length, color, and font.

attribute key

See primary key.

CAD dataset

See CAD feature dataset.

CAD feature dataset

The feature representation of a computer aided design (CAD) file in a geodatabase-enforced schema. A CAD feature dataset is comprised of five read-only feature classes: points, polylines, polygons, multipatch, and annotation. ArcGIS supported formats include DWG (AutoCAD), DXF (AutoDesk Drawing Exchange Format), and DGN (the default Microstation file format).

cartography

The art and science of expressing graphically, usually through maps, the natural and social features of the earth.

check-in

The procedure that transfers a copy of data into a master geodatabase, overwriting the original copy of that data and enabling it so it can be accessed and saved from that location.

checkout

The procedure that records the duplication of data from one geodatabase to another and disables the original data so that both versions cannot be accessed or saved at the same time.

checkout geodatabase

A personal or ArcSDE geodatabase that contains data checked out from a master geodatabase.

checkout version

The data version created in a checkout geodatabase when data is checked out to that database. This version is created as a copy of the synchronization version. Only the edits made to this checkout version can be checked back in to the master geodatabase.

See also checkout geodatabase.

coverage

A data model for storing geographic features. A coverage stores a set of thematically associated data considered to be a unit. It usually represents a single layer, such as soils, streams, roads, or land use. In a coverage, features are stored as both primary features (points, arcs, polygons) and secondary features (tics, links, annotation). Feature attributes are described and stored independently in feature attribute tables. Coverages cannot be edited in ArcGIS 8.3 and subsequent versions.

data

Any collection of related facts arranged in a particular format; often, the basic elements of information that are produced, stored, or processed by a computer.

database management system (DBMS)

A set of computer programs that organizes the information in a database according to a conceptual schema and provides tools for data input, verification, storage, modification, and retrieval.

data model

1. In GIS, a mathematical paradigm for representing geographic objects or surfaces as data. The vector data model represents geography as collections of points, lines, and polygons; the raster data model represents geography as cell matrixes that store numeric values; the TIN data model represents geography as sets of contiguous, nonoverlapping triangles.

2. In ArcGIS, a set of database design specifications for objects in a GIS application. A data model describes the thematic layers used in the application (for example, counties, roads, and hamburger stands); their spatial representation (for example, point, line, or polygon); their attributes; their integrity rules and relationships (for example, streets cannot self-intersect, or counties must nest within states); their cartographic portrayal; and their metadata requirements.

3. In information theory, a description of the rules by which data is defined, organized, queried, and updated within an information system (usually a database management software program).

dataset

Any organized collection of data with a common theme.

DBMS

See database management system (DBMS).

DEM

See digital elevation model (DEM).

digital elevation model (DEM)

The representation of continuous elevation values over a topographic surface by a regular array of z-values, referenced to a common data. Typically used to represent terrain relief.

digital terrain model (DTM)

See digital elevation model (DEM).

disconnected editing

The process of copying data to another geodatabase, editing that data, then merging the changes with the data in the source or master geodatabase.

domain

A group of computers and devices on a network that are administered as a unit with common rules and procedures. Within the Internet, a domain is defined by an Internet protocol (IP) address. All devices sharing a common part of the IP address are said to be in the same domain.

enterprise geodatabase

See multiuser geodatabase.

eXtensible Markup Language (XML)

Developed by the World Wide Web Consortium (W3C), XML is a standard for designing text formats that facilitates the interchange of data between computer applications. XML is a set of rules for creating standard information formats using customized tags and sharing both the format and the data across applications.

feature class

A collection of geographic features with the same geometry type (such as point, line, or polygon), the same attributes, and the same spatial reference. Feature classes can stand alone within a geodatabase or be contained within shapefiles, coverages, or other feature datasets. Feature classes allow homogeneous features to be grouped into a single unit for data storage purposes. For example, highways, primary roads, and secondary roads can be grouped into a line feature class named roads. In a geodatabase, feature classes can also store annotation and dimensions.

feature dataset

A collection of feature classes stored together that share the same spatial reference; that is, they have the same coordinate system, and their features fall within a common geographic area. Feature classes with different geometry types may be stored in a feature dataset.

GDB

See geodatabase (GDB).

geocoding

The process of finding the location of a street address on a map. The location can be an x,y coordinate or a feature such as a street segment, postal delivery location, or building. In GIS, geocoding requires a reference dataset that contains address attributes for the geographic features in the area of interest.

geodatabase (GDB)

A collection of geographic datasets for use by ArcGIS. There are various types of geographic datasets, including feature classes, attribute tables, raster datasets, network datasets, topologies, and so on.

geodatabase data model

The schema for the various geographic datasets and tables in an instance of a geodatabase. The schema defines the GIS objects, rules, and relationships used to add GIS behavior and integrity to the datasets in a collection.

geodataset

Any organized collection of data in a geodatabase with a common theme.

geographic data

Information about real-world features, including their shapes, locations, and descriptions. Geographic data is the composite of spatial data and attribute data.

geographic database

See geodatabase (GDB).

geographic information system (GIS)

An arrangement of computer hardware, software, and geographic data that people interact with to integrate, analyze, and visualize the data; identify relationships, patterns, and trends; and find solutions to problems. The system is designed to capture, store, update, manipulate, analyze, and display the geographic information. A GIS is typically used to represent maps as data layers that can be studied and used to perform analyses.

geometry

The measures and properties of points, lines, and surfaces. In a GIS, geometry is used to represent the spatial component of geographic features. An ArcGIS geometry class is one derived from the Geometry abstract class to represent a shape, such as a polygon or point.

geoprocessing

A GIS operation used to manipulate GIS data. A typical geoprocessing operation takes an input dataset, performs an operation on that dataset, and returns the result of the operation as an output dataset. Common geoprocessing operations are geographic feature overlay, feature selection and analysis, topology processing, raster processing, and data conversion. Geoprocessing allows for definition, management, and analysis of information used to form decisions.

georeferencing

Assigning coordinates from a known reference system, such as latitude/longitude, universal transverse mercator (UTM), or State Plane, to the page coordinates of a raster (image) or a planar map. Georeferencing raster data allows it to be viewed, queried, and analyzed with other geographic data.

GIS

See geographic information system (GIS).

Global Positioning System (GPS)

A constellation of 24 radio-emitting satellites deployed by the U.S. Department of Defense and used to determine location on the earth's surface. The orbiting satellites transmit signals that allow a GPS receiver anywhere on earth to calculate its own location through triangulation. The system is used in navigation, mapping, surveying, and other applications in which precise positioning is necessary.

GPS

See Global Positioning System (GPS).

grid

See raster.

image

A raster-based representation or description of a scene, typically produced by an optical or electronic device, such as a camera or a scanning radiometer. Common examples include remotely sensed data (for example, satellite data), scanned data, and photographs. An image is stored as a raster dataset of binary or integer values that represent the intensity of reflected light, heat, sound, or any other range of values on the electromagnetic spectrum. An image may contain one or more bands.

image catalog

See raster catalog.

key

See primary key.

key attribute

See primary key.

layer

1. In ArcGIS, a reference to a data source, such as a coverage, geodatabase feature class, raster, and so on, that defines how the data should be symbolized on a map. Layers can also define additional properties, such as which features from the data source are included. Layers can be stored in map documents (.mxd) or saved individually as layer files (.lyr). Layers are conceptually similar to themes in ArcView GIS 3.x.

2. A standalone feature class in a geodatabase managed with SDE 3 or ArcSDE.

line

A shape having length and direction but no area, connecting at least two x,y coordinates. Lines represent geographic features too narrow to be displayed as an area at a given scale, such as contours, street centerlines, or streams, or features with no area that form the boundaries of polygons, such as state and county boundary lines.

linear feature

See line.

map

1. A graphic depiction on a flat surface of the physical features of the whole or a part of the earth or other body, or of the heavens, using shapes to represent objects and symbols to describe their nature at a scale whose representative fraction is less than 1:1. Maps generally use a specified projection and indicate the direction of orientation.

2. Any graphical representation of geographic or spatial information.

3. The document used in ArcMap to display and work with geographic data. In ArcMap, a map contains one or more layers of geographic data, contained in data frames, and various supporting map elements, such as a scale bar.

metadata

Information that describes the content, quality, condition, origin, and other characteristics of data or other pieces of information. Metadata for spatial data may document its subject matter; how, when, where, and by whom the data was collected; availability and distribution information; its projection, scale, resolution, and accuracy; and its reliability with regard to some standard. Metadata consists of properties and documentation. Properties are derived from the data source (for example, the coordinate system and projection of the data), while documentation is entered by a person (for example, keywords used to describe the data).

model

1. An abstraction and description of reality used to represent objects, processes, or events.

2. A set of clearly defined analytical procedures used to derive new information from input data.

3. A set of rules and procedures for representing a phenomenon or predicting and outcome. In geoprocessing, a model consists of one process of a sequence of processes connected together. It is created in ModelBuilder or by writing a script using Python and other scripting languages.

4. A data representation of reality, such as the vector data model.

ModelBuilder

A geoprocessing application in ArcGIS used with ArcToolbox to graphically compose a geoprocessing model or script.

multipatch

A type of geometry used to represent the outer surface, or shell, of features that occupy a discrete area or volume in three-dimensional space. They are comprised of planar 3D rings and triangles that are used in combination to model a feature. Multipatches can be used to represent anything from simple to complex objects including spheres, cubes, iso-surfaces, and buildings.

multiuser geodatabase

A geodatabase managed in an RDBMS server by ArcSDE. Multiuser geodatabases can be very large and support multiple, concurrent editors. They are supported on a variety of commercial RDBMSs including Oracle, Microsoft SQL Server, IBM DB2, and Informix.

National Spatial Data Infrastructure (NSDI)

A federally mandated framework of spatial data that refers to U.S. locations as well as the means of distributing and using that data effectively. It includes technologies, policies, standards, and human resources necessary to acquire, process, store, distribute, and improve the utilization of geospatial data in the United States. Developed and coordinated by the Federal Geographic Data Committee (FGDC), the NSDI encompasses policies, standards, and procedures for organizations to cooperatively produce and share geographic data. The NSDI is being developed in cooperation with organizations from state, local, and tribal governments; the academic community; and the private sector.

network

An interconnected set of points and lines that represent possible paths from one location to another. For geometric networks, this consists of edge features, junction features, and the connectivity between them. For network datasets, this consists of edge, junction, and turn elements and the connectivity between them. For example, an interconnected set of lines representing a city streets layer is an example of a network.

NSDI

See National Spatial Data Infrastructure (NSDI).

Oracle

A database company that produces an RDBMS that allows data and other objects to be stored in tables. Oracle provides client/server access to data and uses indexes, sequences, and other database objects to facilitate rapid data creation, editing, and access. ESRI uses Oracle's RDBMS to store vector and raster data for use by ArcSDE.

personal geodatabase

A geodatabase that stores data in a single-user RDBMS. A personal geodatabase can be read simultaneously by several users, but only one user at a time can write data into it.

point

In ESRI software, a type of geometry used to represent point features. A point is defined by a single x,y coordinate pair.

See also point feature.

point feature

In ESRI software, a digital representation of a place or thing that has location but is too small to have area or length at a particular scale, such as a city on a world map or a building on a city map. A point feature may also be used to represent a place or thing that by its nature doesn't have area or length, such as a mountain peak or a lightning strike. Point features have point geometry.

See also point.

polygon

In ESRI software, a type of geometry used to represent polygon features. A polygon is defined by one or more rings, with a ring defined as a path that starts and ends at the same point. A polygon with more than one ring is a multipart polygon. Multipart polygons may be separate or nested, but may not overlap.

See also polygon feature

polygon feature

In ESRI software, a digital representation of a place or thing that has area at a particular scale, such as a country on a world map or a land parcel on a parcel map. Polygon features have polygon geometry.

See also polygon.

polyline

In ArcGIS, a type of geometry used to represent polyline features. A polyline is defined by a set of paths (one or more line segments). If the paths branch or are separate, the polyline is multipart.

See also polyline feature.

polyline feature

In ArcGIS, a digital representation of a place or thing that has length but not area at a particular scale, such as a river on a world map or a street on a city map. Polyline features have polyline geometry.

See also polyline.

primary key

A column or set of columns in a database that uniquely identifies each record. A primary key allows no duplicate values and cannot be NULL.

query

A request that selects features or records from a database. A query is often written as a statement or logical expression.

raster

A spatial data model that defines space as an array of equally sized cells arranged in rows and columns. Each cell contains an attribute value and location coordinates. Unlike a vector structure, which stores coordinates explicitly, raster coordinates are contained in the ordering of the matrix. Groups of cells that share the same value represent the same type of geographic feature.

See also vector.

raster catalog

A collection of raster datasets defined in a table of any format, in which the records define the individual raster datasets that are included in the catalog. A raster catalog is used to display adjacent or overlapping raster datasets without having to mosaic them together into one large file.

RDBMS

Relational database management system. A type of database in which the data is organized across several tables. Tables are associated with each other through common fields. Data items can be recombined from different files. In contrast to other database structures, an RDBMS requires few assumptions about how data is related or how it will be extracted from the database.

relational database management system (RDBMS)

See RDBMS.

relational join

An operation by which two data tables are permanently merged through a common field known as a primary key.

relationship class

An item in the geodatabase that stores information about a relationship. A relationship class is visible as an item in the ArcCatalog tree or contents view.

SDTS

See Spatial Data Transfer Standard (SDTS).

shapefile

A vector data storage format for storing the location, shape, and attributes of geographic features. A shapefile is stored in a set of related files and contains one feature class.

SOAP

Simple Object Access Protocol. An XML-based protocol developed by Microsoft, Lotus, and IBM for exchanging information between peers in a decentralized, distributed environment. SOAP allows programs on different computers to communicate independently of operating system or platform by using the World Wide Web's HTTP and XML as the basis of information exchange. SOAP is now a W3C specification.

See also eXtensible Markup Language (XML).

spatial data

1. Information about the locations and shapes of geographic features and the relationships between them, usually stored as coordinates and topology.

2. Any data that can be mapped.

Spatial Data Transfer Standard (SDTS)

A data exchange format for transferring different databases between dissimilar computing systems, preserving meaning and minimizing the amount of external information needed to describe the data. All federal agencies are required to make their digital map data available in SDTS format upon request, and the standard is widely used in other sectors.

SQL

See Structured Query Language (SQL).

streaming

A technique for transferring data, usually over the Internet, in a real-time flow as opposed to storing it in a local file first. Streaming allows large multimedia files to be viewed before the entire file has been downloaded to a client's computer. When received by the client (local computer), the data is decompressed and displayed using software designed to interpret and display the data rapidly.

Structured Query Language (SQL)

A syntax for defining and manipulating data from a relational database. Developed by IBM in the 1970s, SQL has become an industry standard for query languages in most relational database management systems.

table

1. A set of data elements arranged in rows and columns. Each row represents an individual entity, record, or feature, and each column represents a single field or attribute value. A table has a specified number of columns but can have any number of rows.

2. In ArcView GIS 3.x, one of the five types of documents that can be contained within a project file. A table stores attribute data.

text modifier

See attribute.

tool

1. A geoprocessing operator in ArcGIS that performs specific geoprocessing tasks such as clip, split, erase, or buffer. A tool can belong to any number of toolsets and/or toolboxes.

2. A command that requires interaction with the user interface before an action is performed. For example, with the Zoom In tool, a user must click or draw a box over the geographic data or map before it is redrawn at a larger scale. Tools can be added to any toolbar.

topology

In geodatabases, the arrangement that constrains how point, line, and polygon features share geometry. For example, street centerlines and census blocks share geometry, and adjacent soil polygons share geometry. Topology defines and enforces data integrity rules (for example, there should be no gaps between polygons). It supports topological relationship queries and navigation (for example, navigating feature adjacency or connectivity), supports sophisticated editing tools, and allows feature construction from unstructured geometry (for example, constructing polygons from lines).

transaction

1. A group of data operations that comprise a complete operational task, such as inserting a row into a table.

2. A logical unit of work as defined by a user. Transactions can be data definition (create an object), data manipulation (update an object), or data read (select from an object).

vector

1. A coordinate-based data model that represents geographic features as points, lines, and polygons. Each point feature is represented as a single coordinate pair, while line and polygon features are represented as ordered lists of vertices. Attributes are associated with each feature, as opposed to a raster data model, which associates attributes with grid cells.

2. Any quantity that has both magnitude and direction.

See also raster.

vector product format (VPF)

A standard format, structure, and organization for large geographic databases that are based on a georelational data model.

version

In geodatabases, an alternative state of the database that has an owner, description, permission (private, protected, or public), and parent version. Versions are not affected by changes occurring in other versions of the database.

VPF

See vector product format (VPF).

VPF dataset

See vector product format (VPF).

VPF feature class

See feature class.

XML

See eXtensible Markup Language (XML).